ENGAGING
YOUR TEEN'S WORLD

ENGAGING
YOUR TEEN'S WORLD

Becoming a Culturally Savvy Parent

BRIAN HOUSMAN

BrazosPress

a division of Baker Publishing Group
Grand Rapids, Michigan

© 2009 by Brian Housman

Published by Brazos Press
a division of Baker Publishing Group
P.O. Box 6287, Grand Rapids, MI 49516-6287
www.brazospress.com

Printed in the United States of America

Library of Congress Cataloging-in-Publication Data
Housman, Brian, 1970–
    Engaging your teen's world : become a culturally savvy parent / Brian Housman.
       p. cm.
    Includes bibliographical references.
    ISBN 978-1-58743-254-5 (pbk.)
       1. Parenting—Religious aspects—Christianity. 2. Child rearing—Religious aspects—Christianity. 3. Parent and teenager—Religious aspects—Christianity. I. Title.
BV4529.H67 2009
248.8′45—dc22
                                         2009012609

To Mona,
For allowing me to show you
my whole heart
and still not running away

Contents

Acknowledgments 9

Introduction 11

Part 1 Engaging Your Teen's Culture

1. Friday the 13th 19
2. A Taller Wall, a Wider Moat 27
3. Finger Pointing 41
4. A Big Horse with a Small View 51
5. You against the World? 61

Part 2 Engaging Your Teen's Heart

6. The Writing on the Bedroom Wall 73
7. You Will If It Kills Me 93
8. A Passionate Story 107
9. Hello, I'm a Mac 121

Part 3 Engaging the World Together

10. Melted Gummi Bears 137
11. Boating Upstream 151
12. Employed by Playboy 161
13. When "I Don't Know" Is the Only Honest Answer 181

Group Discussion Guide 187

Notes 199

Acknowledgments

I don't think I had any idea what I was getting into when I started this project. Now I understand why so many writers and artists are mentally unstable. Writing saps your focus for anything else. Or maybe I'm just the weird one that can't write and chew gum at the same time.

Through this whole experience my family—Mona, Bailey, and Ashlan—have put up with me holing up behind a locked door for hours every day. Over the years our family has been through some crazy experiences together and yet they have been willing to follow me on every outlandish adventure. It must be love.

There have been many people that have come alongside me to offer advice, wisdom, and counsel during this project. Thank you to Toby Simers, Brian Briley, and Chris Pekary for allowing me to probe your own lives and experiences. I appreciate the brokenness and transparency with which you live, and I hope I am a few steps further down that road because of your influence. Thank you to Rick Rusaw for your professional advice on writing and the inside scoop on the publishing world.

Thank you to Sarah Parbury, Mona Housman, and Ari Morris for handling my initial writings with care while giving honest feedback and criticism. I wish I could pay you all what you deserve.

A big thank-you to Lisa Ann Cockrel and Rodney Clapp at Brazos Press for taking a chance on an unknown writer. Thanks, Lisa, for going to bat for this project and answering all my rookie questions. I have no idea why Rodney would agree to edit a book for a first-time writer, but you've done a great job making me sound like a better writer than I probably am.

Thank you to the board members of Awake to Life, both present and past, that have helped me stay on this chosen course. I would never have been able to continue on this journey were it not for your encouragement, prayers, challenges, and financial support.

Thanks to my own parents, Wayne and Sheri, for providing a foundation in my own life. I have been blessed to have parents that not only loved me but taught me how to love others.

A special thank-you goes to Steve Collums for being a mentor, counselor, and friend. I've never had a conversation with you when I wasn't challenged. You have spurred my heart and mind to look at my faith as something that daily converges with my culture. Though merely a pilgrim in progress, I've never met anyone whose life reflected 1 Corinthians 11:1 as much as yours, "Follow my example, as I follow the example of Christ" (NIV).

Lastly, thank you to every parent that has come to one of the Parent Summit Conferences, school presentations, or family camps over the years. It has been an honor to be a part of your families and to hear so many of your stories. Many of the thoughts in this book have come out of my times with you. I hope these pages are an accurate representation of both the difficulties and joys you face as parents.

Introduction

Your teen is now living in a postmodern culture. That fact is undeniable. The debate is no longer whether or not we inhabit a postmodern culture. A more fruitful debate is, "Since we are living in a postmodern culture, how will this affect the lives of our teens as they grow older, as well as our families as we engage the culture?" It affects your teen's understanding of relationships, spirituality, justice, and truth—all important characteristics of postmodernism. Their expression of these qualities can look markedly different from what we are used to as parents. Moreover, our unfamiliarity with this new culture can lead to uneasiness in moving into it.

But move into it we must. Author Robert Lewis said, "I believe we need to accept the fact that the world has dramatically changed. We need to recognize, and not ignorantly fight against what is inevitable. If we could finally accept change, we could begin to look at, and not ignore, the issue of postmodernism."[1]

I am not writing in defense of postmodernism or in opposition to it. I am merely attempting to shed light on the adolescent culture as it is today. My intention is not to get bogged down in a heated philosophical debate over the tenets of a postmodern worldview. As a matter of fact, after this introduction you won't see the "p-word" mentioned anymore. Instead, a simple understanding that the perspective of the world I'm describing is from that of a postmodern teenager will be all that is necessary.

There is much of postmodernism that should give us pause. On one hand, this generation feels it is acceptable (and important) to find more meaningful ways to express truth. And this is a good thing. Nonetheless, we have a responsibility to ensure that the conclusions are indeed true, vetted with logic, reason, and scripture, and tempered with tradition.

Consider religion as an example. There are some in evangelical circles who would say that postmodernism is a humanistic and faithless philosophy. While postmodernism does place a greater emphasis on the human experience, it is filled with faith. Admittedly, that faith may look very different from what a Christian traditionalist would consider true faith. I recently watched an NBC News podcast[2] about faith in America that had two interesting observations. One, America is the most religiously diverse nation in the world. Two, for the first time since the founding of America, Catholic Christians will soon be its largest religious group.

Postmodernism indeed has shown a change in religious expression in America, a change that continues to grow. Sociologist Tony Campolo foresees that in the coming years, "the ways in which religion is expressed and the structures that institutionalize it probably will be displaced or changed."[3] He goes on to say that for this new generation of Christians, "the worship of God need not take place in churches that have Episcopalian, Presbyterian, or congregational forms of polity."[4] In other words, where, when, and how this generation expresses their faith in Christ will look very different from what may seem normal to us.

Religion is just one area of transformation among many. As you will see, every area of life is changing for this generation. Moreover, our unfamiliarity with the changes in this new culture can lead to parental uneasiness and unwillingness to adapt to better lead our teens.

We become like the culturally paralyzed private detective, Adrian Monk, from the TV show *Monk*. Although Monk looks normal, he is obsessive compulsive and suffers from multiple phobias. At times Monk's phobias become so deeply incapacitating he is unable to appreciate the fresh air of a walk down the street without fears of accidental disaster at every footstep. He can't enjoy the companionship of others without feeling he will be infected with some unseen disease. Day after day he is forced to make his surroundings fit his view of normalcy, even if that means compulsively touching each parking meter as he walks by it.

This gentle and well-meaning man is genuinely concerned for the people around him but never able to fully engage them, because of his fears and rigid ideas of what makes life right. Instead of experiencing a satisfaction with his job, his family, or even himself, he isolates himself from the world around him.

In many ways, the Christian community today is filled with religious (Adrian) Monks. You love your teen and you want God's best for them. But how they think and the things they say they believe make no sense and seem contrary to how you were raised. As you look at their world a sense of paranoia, fear, or defensiveness wells up inside you. Maybe you feel a need to protect yourself (and your teen) from the confusion and disorder in their changing world without ever stopping to understand what is bringing about the changes.

The good news is that over time, Adrian Monk has gotten a little better. He's become tempered. He's able to see reality more clearly. There's a change taking place in his life, just as there is in your relationship with your teen.

Hopefully, this book will serve as a good place for you to begin to look into some of the changes your teen is likely already exploring. To make our conversation together flow a little easier, I've broken the book into three parts, with a group discussion guide at the end of the book.

Part 1 deals with unhealthy approaches to teen culture that many of us experience as parents. Every day we make choices as to how we will react to the world. Our responses are positions that many of our teens will adopt as they get older. If you respond with anger or disdain, chances are good that your teen will grow up with the same bent toward the world. Likewise, if you model a Christ-honoring response, they too learn how to walk wisely in their culture. But before you can do that, you may have to come face-to-face with your own responses that keep people at a distance.

Part 2 takes you on a journey of discovery into who your teenager really is. It's not important for you to understand all teenagers—just your own. We'll be looking at three different parts of your kids' lives:

1. Their values and how they make decisions;
2. Their passions and how they direct their energies;
3. Their influences and how you can make a greater impact in their lives.

Once you understand healthy ways to respond to a teen's culture, and you understand who your teen is, then you are ready to move into the world together to love others. This is what Part 3 is all about. If this seems like the most difficult part to you, don't worry. It is for me, too. Most of the time we engage our culture by accident or when forced to—like when our teens get into trouble or are in danger. Rarely do we think through ways to intentionally engage the world as a lifestyle of our faith.

The hope here is that the stories and words on these pages will stimulate you to think of ways your family can begin to purposefully love those around you. Just as your teen is part of a culture that is trying to live in a different way, you too must think of ways to move into the culture alongside your family.

As a word of advice, this book may not be most effective if you read it straight through in one sitting. At some points, you may have to put it down and just spend some time thinking. Take time to process what you are reading. Ask the Holy Spirit to show you how to respond in appropriate ways, as well as how to filter what you may disagree with as you continue in the process of making sense of the changing world of your teen.

PART 1

ENGAGING YOUR TEEN'S CULTURE

1

Friday the 13th

There are very few monsters who warrant the fear we have of them.

André Gide[1]

Such love has no fear because perfect love expels all fear.

1 John 4:18

When I was ten years old, my family got cable television for the first time. It lasted about two years in our household. I don't know why my folks got rid of it. I think it had more to do with the cost than the hours wasted watching it. I remember sneaking into the living room late at night, being drawn to the images behind the static snow of the premium channels we hadn't paid for. It may have been fuzzy and jumpy at best, but to a ten-year-old it was still the best sex ed around.

"Where do you think you're going?" my mom said as she saw my brother and me sneaking toward the living room. "You can't go in there tonight, because your dad is watching a grown-up movie." The movie was *Friday the 13th*. I know—it's campy and the gore is juvenile by today's standards, but for 1980 it was the top dog of scary films.

A little later Mom abandoned her post, and I managed to sneak to the wooden, louvered doors that closed off the living room. The slats were slightly open. With the top and bottom of my view cut off by the slats, I was experiencing the first widescreen TV. I stood silently and soaked in every scream and desperate run through the woods. I could feel the tension building but told myself, "This isn't scary. I can handle it. What's the big deal?" Then it happened. Jason (the killer) jumped an unsuspecting victim from behind and lopped off his head. I tripped over my own legs sprinting down the hall to my mom's bedroom. And I added a new emotion to my TV viewing experience—*fear*.

I will not bore you, but if I wanted to, I could tell you similar stories of the first time I watched a couple making out, or glimpsed a naked woman, or heard new curse words, or saw a person beaten to death with a bat—all on TV. Those kinds of things stick with you as a kid.

Turn on your TV at any given time, and you can't miss them. Images. Thousands of them every hour. I read a report the other day that said the typical kid sees 200,000 graphically violent images on TV before he leaves for college.[2] Since I can't think of anything I've done 200,000 times, it sounds like a big number to me. And before you jump to any conclusions, I'm not one of those parents that threw out the family TV years ago. My kids, just like the ones down the street, have grown up watching their fair share of cable TV, playing video games, and singing along with *American Idol* hopefuls.

20

It's not so much TV itself that worries me. It's more the overall values and lifestyle of the culture that the entertainment industry portrays. It's practically an everyday occurrence to hear a network news story of another celebrity (like Britney or Lindsay) whose lifestyle of excess has led him or her into rehab. The video games of the simplistic Mario Bros. have been replaced by the ultraviolent and sadistic likes of Manhunt. Shootings have become an almost expected part of school life. And to top it off, every sitcom seems to make fun of married people and display easy sex without consequences.

When I see things like this, several questions immediately arise. Here are some of the questions that often scroll across my mental screen:

—How bad is it going to get?

—Why do they act so violent?

—How can I protect my kid?

—Has no one ever taught them right from wrong?

—Why don't the authorities do anything about this?

—When are parents going to wake up?

—I wonder if my kid would do that, think that, want that?

Sound familiar? Maybe you have the same questions when it comes to thinking about our teenagers and popular culture as we now know it.

At first glance, these are not bad questions. But they may not be the best questions for parents who want real answers. They don't go far enough or probe deeply enough into the root issues. For example, when you ask, "How can I protect my son or daughter from being influenced by their culture," what are you really asking? Do you want to protect them from getting hurt? Or from experiencing ridicule? Or from facing consequences for poor choices? What are your real fears on behalf of your teen? Let's admit it, many of us are fearful of anything our kids see or hear that leaves us (and our experiential, parental wisdom) out of consideration. Too often our fears come from an almost total lack of understanding about the situation.

I know we live in a world where we say everyone is equal and that it is wrong to judge or stereotype others, but that's just not reality if you think about it. We judge entire groups of people based on the actions of one representative. We presume to know someone's intentions based on their politics, gender, sexual orientation, race, or religion. We do the same thing when it comes to culture. I imagine you recognize common assumptions like these:

—Hollywood has a hedonistic worldview agenda.

—Celebrities are politically liberal.

—Abortion is a choice of convenience.

—Rock stars have no morals.

—Homosexuals are godless pagans.

These are assumptions that many Christians make about entire groups based on the actions of some within those groups. I don't deny my own disappointment in many of our celebrities, social shapers, or politicians, but I am still not given liberty to assume to know the heart or values of each and every one.

Each of these judgments, assumptions, and questions—whether they are fair and accurate or not—leads to emotions. Fear. Frustration. Sadness. Anger. Hate. Excitement. I'm sure you've felt each of these at some point as a result of something you've seen or heard in your teen's culture. And emotions in turn inevitably lead to actions. There is always a response.

It's a natural step from emotion to action. Our actions aren't made in a vacuum. They originate deep down, from our presuppositions and perceptions about the world we live in.

When It All Crashes In

Recently a friend recommended that I watch a film entitled *Crash*. The movie shows what can happen in the human experience when the lives of people from all different walks of life coincide—or collide—during a single day. One character, an older Pakistani man, owns a five-and-dime shop. He thinks no one can be trusted and everyone is trying to cheat him out of a dollar, so he buys a gun. Later, when his store is burglarized, he assumes the burglar was the Latino locksmith who had put in a new lock on the back door to his store. He works up so much anger that he seeks out the locksmith at his home to kill him. His prejudice causes emotion, and that emotion results in action.

Look at the cycle of where this character's presuppositions led him.

Presupposition	*People can't be trusted.*
Question	*How can I protect myself?*
Emotion	*FEAR*
Action	*Reinforce the locks.*
Presupposition	*Latinos are thieves.*
	My burglar must be the Latino locksmith.
Question	*Why would he do this to me?*
Emotion	*RAGE*
Action	*Murder/Revenge*

The presupposition-through-action cycle the shop owner goes through is the same sort of cycle each of us goes through every day. Think about how this cycle plays itself out in your response (action) toward your teen's culture. All the emotions you experience when you think about your teen's world provoke an action. These actions are going to be a factor in the health of the relationship you have with your teen, as well as how you teach him or her to interact with teen culture and the rest of God's world.

Soaking It All In

I've heard many exasperated parents say to me, "If I can just get my kids through their teenaged years, then they'll be okay." There have been many tiring and frustrating days when I could give that sentiment a big thumbs-up. But I think you would agree that "just making it through" wouldn't exactly qualify as a lofty goal—as if somehow the goal of parenting is just to protect or tolerate and then hope for the best. For one thing, that approach doesn't take into account what we might call the sponge effect.

Last year, our daughter got a package of animal-shaped bathtub sponges as a gift. They were each the size of a large multi-vitamin. She dropped one in the sink, and we all watched as it started to grow. Within a few minutes it was the size of her hand. The sponge seemed to just keep soaking and soaking. And once it grew to its full size, it never shrank back to its original size again.

That is what teens are like. They are not just trying to "make it through" a few adolescent years. They are soaking up everything in their environment. And they learn first and foremost through their experiences with you. If you have always responded to people in our culture out of fear, your teen will tend to do the same. If you respond with anger, so will your teen. If you model a disdain for the people that make up your culture, your teen may also.

Not responding to your teen's world is not an option. You will respond, one way or another. But how you respond is entirely up to you. The first step in understanding a teenager's world is making sure your response is based on reality and not on unfounded or unhealthy assumptions. It will require more than sneaking an occasional peek through louvered doors for you to detect and understand the reality of your teenager's world. You'll have to come out from behind any hiding place, fling open the doors, and walk into that world. Then you'll have to explore it patiently and thoroughly, with eyes and ears wide open—only so can you equip yourself for a true and faithful response to your teen's world.

2

A Taller Wall, a Wider Moat

No fear. No distractions. The ability to let that which does not
matter truly slide.

Chuck Palahniuk, *Fight Club*[1]

While I was in middle school, our youth group went to a camp
in Michigan. I remember loving the games and meeting several
girls that I thought might make a good wife one day. There
was a waterslide that took my breath away. And I thought my
counselor was the coolest guy I'd ever met. My friends and I
played practical jokes on each other and drank Coke floats.
In short, we did the sorts of things kids do at any camp. But
when the hundreds of campers came together for the evening
worship service, things turned weird.

We got yelled at. A lot. For the life of me, I can't recall what we had done wrong.

One of the things I remember blasted from the stage is that Jesus wanted me to have Christian friends, and lots of them. My school friends would pull me away from God, so I needed to stick close to my church friends. The well-intentioned but extremely intense speaker said that when we got home from this spiritual mountaintop, the enemy would be after us. He would use every trick in his bag to trip us up, so we should protect ourselves. And obviously (according to the speaker) the devil's biggest tricks to throw us off our spiritual track would be rock music, movies, and girls. At least that's what my seventh-grade ears heard.

It all sounded convincing, not to mention emotionally stirring. And loud. The world was waiting to pounce on me when I least expected it, but as long as I protected myself from the evil music, evil movies, and evil girls, everything would be okay. So I protected myself . . . except from the girls. I was thirteen and just warming up to the idea of girls being a good thing. I wasn't about to write them off that quickly, no matter how much that guy yelled!

Looking back now, it makes sense that it was so confusing. The speaker had an orientation toward culture rooted in fear, born from a common presupposition that many Christians embrace. It's a belief that most of our culture is basically evil, so you have to protect yourself (and your kids) from it.

Now you could already be thinking, "How could that possibly be a wrong presupposition?" So I'm asking you for a little grace and space to explain. In the end, you might still disagree. And that's okay, it's just one chapter among many. But I believe facing your fears, whether real or imagined, head-on, instead of building a wall because of them, will greatly change how you view culture and help bring better understanding and grace to your teen's world.

Back to the Middle Ages

It's a medieval approach to culture. Literally. A thousand years ago the most efficient way for people to protect everything they valued about their way of life was to dig a moat and erect tall stone walls. They built an impenetrable defense around all that they most loved. They thought anyone or anything not like them was against them, so it was to be avoided. A wall was the perfect way to keep it all out.

You can hear the same warlike, defensive language coming from many Christian teachers. The posture of fear seems so strong that at times it's as if William Wallace—Braveheart himself—is on the stage telling us to take up arms to protect our women and children and homes. This defensive posture toward culture is what author Spencer Burke refers to as a boundary model for life. He says, "Boundary models are likely to be riddled with fear and suspicion toward those who live on the 'outside.' The church is filled with people who value the faith, and for the sake of what they think is faith, they despise culture and all that it means."[2]

Imagine yourself as one who is outside the church. You are not averse to God and see the goodness in many Christians. You want to find out more about why these people are so committed to living differently. Out of curiosity you decide to attend a church service in your community. And as you sit to listen, you hear things such as:

—Hollywood stars are luring our kids with a lifestyle of excess, and we must fight against them.
—The depravity of homosexuality is destroying traditional family values. We must fight against it.
—Music entertainers are deceiving teens into a behavior of casual sex, and we must fight against them.

Remember, you have come to learn and understand. Might you conclude that Christians think everyone is out to get them? Or that they are intolerant? Or that they are very angry people? Would you honestly leave feeling drawn to their picture of Jesus or way of life? After hearing their message would you be willing to commit yourself to being a part of their spiritual community?

Let me be clear. There are many damaging and conflicting messages in pop culture. In many regards there is a world-view that is unhealthy and even flat-out deadly. For example, I have noticed that the lifestyle of excess my children view as they watch Hollywood pop stars and professional athletes in the media has made it difficult to teach my own kids to resist excess and to develop hearts of gratitude. Pop culture also contains many examples of rampant violence, promiscuous sexuality, and disregard for authority. Like you, I get frustrated with seeing our culture move further and further away from God's design for peaceful living, healthy sexuality, and right use of our possessions. But here's the difference: *In no way do I view the people in the culture as my enemy or the enemy of my family.*

Recognize the Right Enemy

To be sure, we do have an enemy, but it is not human. Your frustration, anger, and fight has to be directed toward the one who deserves it, not against others who, like you, are made in God's image. The apostle Paul tells us clearly who our enemy is.

Put on all of God's armor so that you will be able to stand firm against all strategies of the devil. For *we are not fighting against flesh-and-blood enemies, but against evil* rulers and authorities of the unseen world, against mighty powers in this dark world, and against evil spirits in the heavenly places. (Eph. 6:11–12)

The gluttony, the distortion of family, the sexual promiscuity, and the glorification of violence in popular culture are all "strategies and tricks of the Devil." It is not the people who do these things that are your enemy. It is the one who has deceived them that we war against. This truth has huge implications for your relationships (and your teen's) with people in your community. Maybe you are like some who started their fight against a cultural worldview that trivializes sin but are now fighting against the very people around you.

And don't let yourself settle for the cliché we've all heard to "love the sinner but hate the sin." This has proven time and again to be a disingenuous means for Christians to say we receive people, while actually stiff-arming them to keep them away. We keep our distance to prevent ourselves from being "tainted by the world." But in reality this response keeps us from getting involved or having to care about what is happening in our world. Yes, it is our world too. As Derek Webb sang, "I can't deny this fallen world; though not my home it's where I live. How can I preserve and light the way for a world that I can't admit I'm in?"[3]

I was recently speaking on faith and culture at a church. It was a very intense presentation on the state of youth culture. For an hour I laid out many of the unhealthy influences in the lives of teenagers, potentially destructive life-changing decisions teens are making, and how there isn't much of a difference statistically between Christian and non-Christian teens in their behavior and lifestyle choices. At the end I offered to take questions. Big mistake. A gentleman raised his hand and began to speak—not question, just speak.

"I hear what you're saying, but I believe we live in an evil culture. I believe we are in a fight with the world. I think we have to be prepared to go to war against them."

He went on to explain that his own family had chosen to homeschool so that he could train his children to learn to fight against the culture around them. I don't mean to make any pronouncements about homeschooling in general, but for this particular dad, schooling his own children was his opportunity to train up his children to be prepared for the great cultural evils confronting them. It was an "us against them."

I've been speaking to parent groups for several years and love hearing their stories and comments, but I don't think I've ever heard a response that disturbed me more than this one. For days I couldn't focus on anything else but the remarks of this genuinely concerned father. I feel for him, with his fear for the safety of his kids. He is ready to battle "the world" for their sake. But mostly, I hurt for him and, at the heart of him, his contempt for the "them" he sees in our culture.

The only contempt Jesus ever showed toward *people* was toward the religious ones that did not live according to the values of God's kingdom. His anger was directed toward those who failed to genuinely love God or to love other people. Their response to people whose lifestyles they reviled was to pick up rocks and rage against them. The response of Jesus was altogether different. His response was to love, to spend time with, to touch, and to esteem their value as people.

The Time Is Now

One of my favorite scriptures is from the apostle Paul, "But when the right time came, God sent his Son . . ." (Gal. 4:4). It always makes me wonder why then was the perfect time. I've heard suggestions like the system of Roman roads made it easy to spread the gospel, or that the earlier reign of Alexander the Great created a unifying culture and language, or that the Old Testament was completed. I'm sure these were all factors, but maybe we make it more complex than it is. Maybe it's as simple as this: God was tired of religious people confusing his plan, so he sent Jesus to be the living picture of how to love and receive love, how to value and honor one another.

Maybe the time has fully come for us as well. Maybe it's time to decide that we will move toward people in our world the way Jesus did, with great love and concern for the culture.

Think for a moment about how you approach the culture around you (and how you've taught your teen to do the same) as you read these words from Jesus's first big public speech. These words set the tone for the next three years of his life and work.

> God blesses those who are humble, for they will inherit the whole earth. God blesses those who hunger and thirst for justice, for they will be satisfied. God blesses those who are merciful, for they will be shown mercy. God blesses those whose hearts are pure, for they will see God. God blesses those who work for peace, for they will be called the children of God. (Matt. 5:5–9)

Jesus is saying he desires a different quality to our relationships. Yes, Jesus came to save us from sin for all of eternity, but his coming also had an immediate purpose—to make things right. The kingdom he envisions for us to be part of is one characterized by gentleness, a thirst for justice, mercy, and working toward peace. That doesn't mean we don't resist manipulative advertising toward teens or hold the entertainment culture accountable for its errant messages. But it does mean we had better do so with mercy and a recognition that even "evil advertisers" are made in the image of God. We do not have permission to respond with indignation and anger toward others, unless our hearts are first willing to be broken for them.

I once had the opportunity to deliver the keynote address at the state PTA conference in Tennessee. Here I was speaking before an organization that many in the church would consider socially and educationally liberal. But that's not at all what I found. As I spoke of the empty messages of our entertainment industry and the destructiveness of the choices many teens make, this room with hundreds of moms had a more appropriate spiritual response than I've seen in most churches. They were broken. I saw moms weeping. Moms who had to leave the room to gather their composure. Moms who wanted prayer for their families.

I suggested to these concerned parents that they could not be angry at Eminem or the Pussycat Dolls, not at least until their hearts were first broken for them. These PTA parents didn't open their hearts to anger or indignation that day. There was no room for it. Instead, there was an appropriate sadness. Sadness at the destructive choices the entertainers can make. And brokenness for their own teens when they had embraced those destructive messages.

The reaction of these parents reminded me very much of how Jesus responded as he stood on the hillside overlooking the great city of Jerusalem. He was sad about Jerusalem's unbelief, and broken as he witnessed the self-destructiveness of the city. Even when he hung on a cross, condemned there by men more concerned with maintaining religious control than living a surrendered life, he didn't condemn the common people who had given into the frenetic energy of the moment and began casting stones and shouting taunting remarks out of ignorance. Both his message and actions were of embrace.

It takes only a cursory look at the stories of Jesus to see a person who knew that others needed to be *loved first*, before trying to address unhealthy actions in their lives. Jesus sees a cowardly and crooked man in a tree and says to him, "Zac-

34

chaeus, I want to go to your house." Early one afternoon, Jesus sees a woman at a well who has stumbled into adultery, and he says, "I can give you what you seek, what you truly need." Whether it was a Roman military officer, a leprous man, or a harlot, Jesus's first response was to embrace and love. Time and again, those that the religious establishment rejected, Jesus received.

Jesus proactively moved into the culture of his day to make right that which had been broken by sin. The only way he chose to change the lives around him was to open himself to others, and in doing so to illuminate their brokenness and his healing. Theologian H. Richard Niebuhr wisely observed, "To mankind, with his perverted nature and corrupted culture, Jesus Christ has come to heal and renew what sin has infected . . . by revelation and instruction he reattaches the soul to God, the source of its being and goodness, and restores to it the right order of love."[4]

Hang on to some of those words for a moment. *Renew. Reattaches. Restores.* There was an intentionality to Jesus's interactions with his culture. Surely it was uncomfortable at times to see the brokenness of the world, to see the shame that sin brings, and still choose to move toward others because he knew the possibilities of what a relationship with him could bring to their lives.

There is a scene in one of the *Chronicles of Narnia* by C. S. Lewis that involves a bratty boy named Eustace. On a particularly difficult part of his journey with the Pevensie children, Eustace begins to whine and complain about his circumstances and wanders away from his friends. He comes upon a cave full of riches and decides to take the treasure as his own. Because of this act of selfishness, he is turned into a dragon. After several days his friends are frantically searching for him, afraid that something tragic has happened. Searching a beach for

Eustace, they encounter a dragon. Upon seeing the children, the dragon begins to wildly flap its wings and blow smoke from its nostrils. The children panic. Some run away and others take up swords to defend themselves. All respond defensively except one—Lucy.

Somehow, Lucy sees a goodness in the dragon. She sees his flapping and snorting not as an attack, but rather a plea for help. She sees a brokenness and hurt in his spirit. She sees past the scales and claws to something deeper. She alone sees the frightened boy inside who is desperate to be free from his hideous exterior.

Similarly, several years ago I had the privilege of working with a group of volunteers that saw something deeper in the lives of teenagers than the occasional ugliness of their popular culture. I was working as a youth pastor at a church that owned camp facilities in the Ozark Mountains. Every fall the church would sponsor outreach camps designed for students to invite their friends from school. This was not an outreach camp in name only, where no one really brought their friends. Instead hundreds of unchurched students would show up. And it had nothing to do with me as their leader. It was a unique time and place where God did something special through a group of teenagers. I've been away from there for a long time, but God continues to bring kids in need of him to that beautiful mountaintop called Castle Bluff.

There I learned that if you're going to do outreach, you had better be ready for what might happen. One time we had a girl dancing through camp with a wire clothes hanger on her head, talking about the great advances of the pro-choice movement. Another time we had guys who were gang members and wanted nothing to do with Bible studies. I remember once sharing the gospel with a dreadlocked guy who smelled strongly of pot (he even wore the stereotypical leather jacket). It was a common practice for volunteers to get little sleep because of having to hunt down campers who had sneaked out of their cabins. Even with all of that, it was also a common experience to see a dozen or more kids give their lives to Christ at the end of the weekend. Think of any type of kid you can, and we saw their lives changed. I don't know that those volunteer leaders (mostly parents) always felt they knew the right thing to say, but I do know I've never seen kids as deeply loved. Year after year, those parents were Jesus to a bunch of teens whose lives were far different from that of their own kids.

That doesn't mean that they (as parents) accepted the unhealthy lifestyles of the campers, any more than Jesus accepted sexual perversion, religious manipulation, or unfair tax practices. But it was never the person he condemned, it was the "strategies and tricks" being used by the enemy in the lives of the people he loved. He didn't offer them protection from the world, but rather freedom from their past sins. He did not dig a moat of safety around them but enabled them to go out and embrace others.

Seeing Truth All Around

As a parent, you have a responsibility to protect your children. It is your job to look out for their best interests. You lead them in such a way that they can discover God's love and design for their lives. That means there are many things, places, and situations you direct them away from in order to protect them from destructive choices.

You do this because you love your teen, not because you hate the world. It's a positive motivation, not a negative one. When you see your two-year-old begin to wander toward the curb as a car approaches, what do you do? You grab him and pull him toward safety, because you love him, not because of an irrational contempt for Chevrolets.

It is one thing to steer your teen toward God's best; it is altogether different to view everyone else as evil if they don't fit into your definition of God's best. Your choices as a parent must be based on what is best for your teen, not on a fear about their culture. You can't assume that since music isn't sung by a Christian, then it must be bad, or that if a movie isn't produced by a Christian movie company, then it must be evil. Instead, judge each situation in your culture based on its potential for redeeming truth.

Probe.

Examine.

Test.

Author and pastor Rob Bell says it this way: "If God is truth and all truth is God's truth, then Jesus takes us into the truth, not away from it. He frees us to embrace whatever is true and good and beautiful wherever we find it."[5] In other words, look closer. There may be truth hidden in the cultural message worth digging out.

A deeper look at some Hollywood films in recent memory provides opportunity to talk about what God considers to be true, right, admirable, and worthy of talking about. *Spider-Man* is a great example of responsibility and the effect one's choices may have on others. *Juno* dealt with the difficulty of teen pregnancy and how to take responsibility for your actions. *Kit Kittredge* showed how to weather hard times as part of a community. *Cinderella Man* was an incredible depiction of integrity and the staying power of family. *Glory Road* showed us both the scars of racism and the strides our country has taken toward equality. And I was personally deeply affected by the portrayal of honor and forgiveness in *The Kite Runner*. Lesser-known independent films like *Dear Frankie*, *The Namesake*, and *Resurrecting the Champ* were honest representations of the difficulties that sometimes accompany being a family. Even if you find instances in each film you disagree with, I believe each is replete with examples of redemptive truth.

It's not just movies where we find this to be true. One of my friends, Jamin, was an art major at the University of Memphis. Going to his art exhibits, one couldn't help but see the struggles of the young artists to express the complexities of the human experience in all of its glory and gore. Reflections of faith, pain, truth, and renewal could be seen all around. Those same struggles can be seen in music, movies, and politics. It would be easy to cast it all out as being too graphic or godless—and consequently miss God's redemption that is taking place.

This is particularly important considering the role pop culture plays in the lives of teens today. Spencer Burke has keenly observed, "Pop culture is the new spiritual environment in our world today."[6] Pop culture, with its music, TV programs, movies, and Web sites, isn't just about entertainment. For teens it is an expression of their relationships, their values, and their spiritual beliefs.

A good example is the recent Live Earth event.[7] Simultaneous events took place on all seven continents featuring speakers and bands that brought awareness to one of the most important issues of this teen generation—environmentalism. Throughout the event, hundreds of thousands text-messaged the commitments they were willing to make to conserve energy, recycle, and use renewable products. During the '60s many music artists were known for their antiwar messages. Today's artists sing about the values of this generation such as social justice, racial equality, globalism, community restoration, and the aforementioned environmentalism. Recognizing that popular culture is the "spiritual environment in our world today" should cause you all the more to mine for truth in pop culture, discerning how its messages resonate with your teen.

Part of your challenge as a parent is to keep a daily heads-up on what is happening in your teens' world and use the media and relational experiences around them to point out truth. For instance, don't just plop down $8.50 for a movie next Friday night. Use it as an opportunity for meaningful conversation later. Engage your son in conversation about the music he listens to and the celebrities he idolizes. Take a walk through the mall with your daughter, observe everything around you, and talk about values of modesty or materialism. Watch the latest sporting-scandal story on ESPN Sports Center with your son, and talk about character issues like integrity and honesty. These teachable moments are around you every day in your culture. Use them. Redeem them.

Instead of running from culture, you can run toward it and see the beauty and truth in it. You can lead your teen into seeing the redemption of God happening, albeit sometimes in small ways, all throughout culture. If you do, the depths of your conversations with your teen will be beyond your expectations.

3

Finger Pointing

If your daily life seems poor, do not blame it; blame yourself, tell yourself that you are not poet enough to call forth its riches.

Rainer Maria Wilke[1]

Blame someone else and get on with your life.

Alan Woods[2]

I remember sitting in church in the eighth grade, listening to a preacher talk about rock music. He kept playing songs backward and then telling us the "hidden messages" in the music. He said the real meaning of the songs could be heard only by those with a steady hand able to rotate the record player in reverse.

My best friend and I were completely confused about what he was saying. For one thing, it was really hard to make sense of Rod Stewart singing backward. For another thing, I don't think either of us were buying it. My friend's dad was somewhat of a cultural liberal in our church, when it came to music. That meant he listened to the Beatles and referred to the sixties as the "glory days of rock music." So we had heard all the songs already and couldn't figure out what was the big deal.

That's when the preacher dropped his bombshell. "It's music like this that's making you kids go out and do drugs." Well, we never sat around doing drugs while listening to Def Leppard, but shortly after this speaker's message, our church had a record-breaking party (except it was with cassette tapes). I'll admit I brought many of my own. I should probably also admit that over the years I've repurchased most of them.

I'm not saying the effects of music can be ignored. Music is a significance influence in the lives of many teens. And I think there is a lot of music peddled today that is a waste of shelf space (especially as far as musical quality goes). Furthermore, I disagree with the worldview messages of much of today's pop music. Much of it sends conflicting messages to teens about their sexuality, how to deal with emotions, and the value of authority. But while music may give me insight into the values of the teen culture, I don't blame it for the state of our culture.

I'm of the opinion that you can't blame music for teen drug use any more than you can blame Howard Stern for social crudeness, Snoop Dog for gang violence, or Planned Parenthood for teenage abortions. The problems of culture are much more complex than can be expressed in blanket statements like these. Yes, these are all contributing factors in their areas of influences, but all the blame can't be placed squarely at their feet.

One of the workshops I conduct on a regular basis in schools and churches speaks to the typical messages teens receive in pop music. Inevitably, a parent will ask me if I think rap music is bad. Honestly, this is a difficult issue to handle and get parents to understand. My answer is no, rap music is not bad. But here's the deeper issue: I believe rap music's general messages about women are degrading and dehumanizing. Much of it glorifies violence toward others, particularly authority figures. A lifestyle of greed and gluttony is encouraged and exploited many times over. But we must be careful to identify the evil in the message and not blame the art form itself.

I know it's frustrating as a parent when you are trying to figure out why your teen is respectful and listens to advice one day, and the next day treats you like a reality show castoff. You may start looking around to find something to blame, something to pinpoint for your teen's behavior. But rarely is it a single influence, like a certain genre of music. There's a deeper dynamic at work, and music is symptomatic of it.

Banning Barbie

I was enjoying a quiet moment with a book when our daughter Ashlan, who was five years old at the time, came in with a question. "Hey, Daddy, do you know the song that goes, 'Hit me baby one more time'?" As she moved her hips in perfect pop idol fashion, all I could muster was a stunned, "Uh, yeah." What I was really thinking was, "How in the world did my five-year-old learn a Britney Spears song?"[3]

It took another week for my answer to come.

Ashlan was into Polly Pocket at the time and wanted me to guide her to the Web site. Polly Pocket is a micro version of Barbie, and as I found out on the Web site, made by the same company—Mattel. Once we got to the site, I noticed an obvious link to other products made by Mattel.

No sooner had I handed the mouse to Ashlan than she clicked on the Barbie link. Not really minding if she looked at Barbie stuff, I sat back and relaxed.

A few minutes later my ears perked up as I heard the familiar words of Britney Spears's hit song ". . . Baby One

More Time." Her lyrics laced with sexually explicit overtones were coming over my computer speakers. And it was Barbie singing it.

I knew that back in the seventies Barbie went disco, and somewhere in the eighties she took off to Malibu, but here she was mesmerizing my five-year-old with her flared jeans, midriff tops, and best dance moves. And she wasn't just singing. She was teaching as the words scrolled by karaoke-style along with the music.

I felt duped. I felt manipulated. And I was. I thought my daughter would be enjoying a few Barbie coloring pages and stories. I had no idea she would be learning about relational/sexual issues that she's not ready to understand. Not in my wildest imagination did I ever envision my five-year-old learning the art of seduction from Britney Spears via Barbie.

I was seething with anger. Not at my daughter, but at Mattel. Mattel was to blame, or more pointedly their Web-site developers. It was their fault little girls were growing up too fast. If it weren't for them, preteen girls wouldn't be acting so sexual.

Maybe this sounds familiar to you. It probably wasn't Barbie or Mattel, but there was some other incident that involved your kid, and you had an easy target for your blame.

—You overheard your eleven-year-old son and his friends telling jokes with sexual overtones they got from TV. That new sitcom he watched last night is to blame.

—You go shopping with your eighth-grade daughter, and all the outfits she picks out make her look like she crawled out of a teen fashion magazine. *Seventeen* is to blame.

—You tell your son that since he didn't do his chores, he can't go out with friends tonight. He responds by yelling and throwing things in his room. It must be the work of those violent video games he plays.

After seeing my daughter sing along with Britney/Barbie, I spent two days being angry at Mattel (as if they cared or even knew). Then I finally had to admit that Mattel was not a great evil entity out to corrupt my daughter. They were just selling dolls and thought Britney Spears would be a good bet to get girls' attention. And it worked. In reality, I was frustrated with myself and was looking for some other place to unload. I was frustrated that I hadn't paid more attention to the Web site. I was frustrated that I had left her alone to explore it. It was my fault.

I don't know about you, but it seems especially hard to admit blame when it comes to my kids' well-being. Surely I'm not part of the problem. It comes down to pride. I want my kids to like me. I want them to think I am cool. And as far as parenting goes, I want them to think better of me than I really am. Hey, I already think more of myself than I should, so why shouldn't they?

I did the same thing when I was a youth pastor. Looking back, I think I was highly ineffective my first five years of ministry, exactly because I was so concerned with doing things that would make students like me. All the good I could have done was stunted by my preoccupation with myself. Plain and simple—it was pride.

Proverbs 29:23 says, "Pride ends in humiliation, while humility brings honor," and I have had the unfortunate privilege of seeing it proven. My pride kept me from listening to constructive criticism from coworkers. Kept me from asking for advice. But the most damaging part was it kept me from taking responsibility.

Pride made it easy for me to say, "It's not my fault." In my mind I couldn't be at fault. It was the lead pastor's fault for not supporting me. It was a parent's fault for complaining about me. It was a volunteer's fault for misunderstanding me. Sometimes it was even a student's fault for not sticking with me. Anyone else was to blame—anyone but me.

I wish I could say I don't struggle with pride anymore, but it's a daily battle. I have to decide if I'll position myself to look good or to love other people. Will the focus be me or others?

You struggle with it, too. Don't you? Be honest. How many of your decisions about your teen are really based on positioning yourself? When is the last time you thought, "What will the other parents think if I let my son go there?" Or better yet, "What will people at church think if I let my daughter do that?" Or worst of all, "How much more will my kid love me if I let them do this?"

Don't worry. I'm right there with you. I struggle with parental pride, too. And when things go wrong, it's pride that keeps me or you from taking responsibility as a parent.

But It's Not His Fault

I saw this over and over again when I worked at a private high school. I was on staff as a spiritual counselor to students, so I was privy to many of the difficulties they were going through. When there was a problem with a student and a parent had to be called, the principal would bring me into the conversation. No matter what the situation, there was a common response from parents.

—One parent was confronted with her son having drugs in his car. "Those can't be his. You can't blame him. You've got the wrong kid."

—A girl got caught passing around a note with horrible rumors about another girl. "This can't be hers. She must have been put up to it. You've got the wrong girl."

—A student was failing math and needed help. "My kid is smart. He wouldn't be doing so poorly if he didn't have such a bad teacher."

I was watching a local news story on school violence in our community. Journalists talked to politicians, community leaders, and principals about the problem. And each one seemed to point the finger in the same direction—at gangs. Admittedly, gangs are a real problem in the schools of Memphis, but there are many other issues—overworked and inattentive parents, absentee fathers, lack of security, or even poor student character development. Unfortunately, I never heard one of the "respected community leaders" take any of the responsibility for the problem. It's easier to blame gang members and move on. It's not like the reporters were going to get gang leaders on the air and ask if they thought they were being characterized fairly by the news media.

This local story isn't an isolated incident. In the past few years there have been stories on all sorts of issues where parents have found someone to blame. Look at these actual newspaper headlines:

Parents Blame Cereal Ads for Childhood Obesity

Too sugary and sweet to resist

Parents Blame Kentucky School Shooting on Hollywood

Who's to blame for the tragedies?

Parents Blame "the Evil Internet" for Daughter's Runaway Marriage

"The Internet made her do it!"

Parents Blame Cannabis for Son's Suicide

Drugs are at fault

Parents Blame Son's Fatal Fall on Video Game

Attempt at skating trick gone horribly wrong

I don't discount the difficulty and pain parents feel in dealing with these situations, but it is almost comical how often these types of headlines can be found in the paper today.

Where is the responsibility on our part as parents? When do we stop and own up to our role in what is happening?

The culture of blame has become such a part of the American way of life that it's made it easy for us to adopt it into our faith as well. Just turn on your local Christian radio station. Many of the talk show hosts have a strong rhetoric of blame. They blame our nation's ills on whatever party is in office or on "liberal" federal judges. Rarely do I hear solutions discussed that require responsibility, brokenness, or repentance on their part. I love the words of folk artist Alice Peacock when she declares, "America the free, wake up from your fantasy. / Is the nation so divided we can't see / That there's work to be done / something there for everyone / I know / I'll start with me."[4]

The bellyaching of some Christians reminds me of the children of Israel when they were in the desert.

A great change had taken place. A shift in their surroundings. They were led by Moses into freedom. A new way of living in community. A rediscovery of their identity and what it means to be God's chosen people. But because of their own actions, they had to get to the land promised them via a trip through the desert. Instead of responding with a broken heart, or at least a willingness to obey in the future, they complained. Or as a friend of mine says, they were "whiney-butts." They blamed Moses when they didn't have food to eat. They blamed Moses when their clothes wore out. They blamed Moses when all they had to drink was bitter water. At one point they even said, "It would be better for us if we were back in Egypt. There we had pots of meat to eat." Pots of meat? Now, that's the ideal life! Sounds like many in today's Christian circles longing for the "good ol' days."

There are two things I've always wondered about the Israelites' story. One, what kind of love did it take for Moses to stay? I can't imagine myself sticking around for forty years listening to all the complaining and accusations. Two, why didn't the people try to make a difference in the quality of their own lives? When they were frustrated over food, why didn't they go look for some on their own? If they felt exposed and unprotected, why not mobilize an army? Instead, their response was to find someone to blame for their poor circumstances.

We should grieve over the loss of innocence in our culture and our inability to blush over the sexualization of every part of life. We should long for wholeness and healthy life choices for our teens. But the answer is not to blame others when we see risky behavior manifest in our own children. This is not the time for blame. It's the time to put our hearts into action.

4

A Big Horse with a Small View

Stupidity has a certain charm—Ignorance does not.

Frank Zappa[1]

Blinding ignorance does mislead us. O! Wretched mortals, open your eyes.

Leonardo da Vinci[2]

I've always wondered who was the first person to decide it was a good idea for man to ride on the back of a horse. Did he (or an industrious nomadic woman) try other animals first? Maybe a zebra or an ox? Apparently, word hadn't made its way to the horse I once tried to ride that his purpose was to support me for an hour as I sat on his back.

I was in seventh grade, on a Saturday afternoon date with my first real girlfriend, Melissa. Melissa liked horses and often went to ride them. Unlike me. As her manly thirteen-year-old boyfriend, I tried to put it over on her that I knew what I was doing. I wasn't fooling myself, but I hoped she wouldn't notice.

Melissa had long, dark brown hair with lots of wavy curls. She looked just like one of those women from shampoo commercials, her hair bouncing in perfect time with the horse's trot.

My horse didn't trot.

If you've ever seen the episode of *Seinfeld* where Elaine tries, with hilarious results, to dance at a party, then you have a pretty good picture of my horse (sans the dress). If I got near a tree, he twisted. If another horse came in sight, he ran. If I went near the road, he spun around. I'll admit I was afraid.

At one point I heard Melissa say, "Horses can tell when you are afraid of them." It's the only time I remember thinking it would be okay to hit a girl.

I learned a couple of things that day. One, no matter how badly I wanted to impress a pretty girl, my horsemanship wasn't going to do it. Two, it all made sense now why so many horses have to wear blinders.

Horses have a tremendous amount of energy. They have the ability to stay focused on a difficult task and keep at it until it's done. We may have made them into beasts of burden, but they are still incredibly graceful and intelligent.

You take this same energetic animal and put blinders on it, and it begins to act almost lifeless. The blinders block the horse's vision so that it's only able to see what is directly in front of it. As far as the horse is concerned, its whole reality is the fifteen degrees of visibility in front of its face.

The Unfathomable

The last parental assumption about teen culture I want to explore is one that has many parents living just like the horse with blinders. However, there is one major difference between the blinders on horses and the figurative blinders worn by parents. A horse's blinders are placed there by the animal's master in order to bring focus, to remove distractions. In contrast, we as parents have cultural blinders that we often intentionally place on our eyes with our own hands. These blinders have the opposite result of horses' blinders. They bring disorientation, confusion, and ignorance.

Many times, parents are unable to honestly address issues in teen culture because they still view their teens as the innocent children they once were. See if you've ever found yourself thinking thoughts like those below. (Again, I'll admit I've done it myself.)

—"My kid is too disciplined to get into drugs."

—"My child is too smart to believe media messages."

—"My teen is too spiritually committed to be sexually active."

—"My daughter is too happy to have an eating disorder."

—"My son is too young to get involved with pornography."

As you take an honest look at youth culture, the most helpful question you can ask yourself is, "Might this be true of my teen?" I'm not saying your kid is having sex, doing drugs, or meeting strangers online—but you must be willing to ask yourself if it might be possible. To ask the question doesn't unfairly bring your teen's character into question, nor does it require you to assume the worst. It simply allows you to continue moving forward in a relationship with him or her, with the possibilities for mishap fully acknowledged.

I was speaking at a conference addressing unhealthy choices among teens. I had just covered some recent statistics on adolescent alcohol usage. I mentioned that according to a new study, 29 percent of high school students binge drink once a month.[3] During the Q&A portion, a dad raised his hand. He said, "I find that figure hard to believe. As you talked, I've done some quick math. That would mean over 80 percent of seniors are binge drinking."

Not wanting to point out what seemed an obvious math error, I asked him to explain his reasoning. "In order for 30 percent of all students to binge drink," he replied, "there would have to be at least 80 percent of seniors binge drinking, since freshmen don't drink." Did you catch that?

This dad was wearing cultural blinders that made him unable to fathom the reality that some freshmen drink alcohol. His rationale made sense after I learned that his own son was in middle school. He couldn't imagine that the high school culture his son was preparing to enter was much more challenging than he had thought.

Over the years, I've counseled with many parents whose teens were involved in some type of unhealthy behavior. Too many times these parents have asked me, "How could this happen?" It may be simplistic to say, "Your inability to believe that it could happen is partly how it happened." But at the very least, it is a factor. Sometimes our worst enemy is our own ignorance. Where teen culture is concerned, let's strive to be innocent as doves, but cunning as serpents.

If you don't think your son would drink and drive, what reason would you have to talk with him about it? If you can't conceive of your daughter having sex with her boyfriend, why would you ever bring up the subject? Our inability to come to grips with the possibility of how our own teens might interact with their culture leaves them having to figure out healthy boundaries on their own. Much of the time, that may not effectively happen.

But I'm Not an Expert

A friend of mine, Chris, was an air force pilot for many years. For vacation a few years ago, our family went to visit his family at their home in Florida. While we were there, Chris treated my wife and me to a flight along the Florida coastline.

I've flown many times in commercial airplanes, but I knew this was going to be a unique experience. The blue of the sky and water could not have been more beautiful as we seemed to float along the beach from above. In our small rental plane, there were many things that could have caused fear. The sudden bumps from shifting air currents. The creaking wings that seemed to almost bounce from time to time. But I never felt really afraid as long as I kept reminding myself, "Chris is an air force pilot. He knows exactly what he is doing." Every part of the experience seemed to be going great until (cue suspense music) I heard Chris say, "Here, you fly awhile."

Surely he'd said, "There's a fly on the wall," or maybe, "It's flying well." But when he removed his hands from the yoke, leaned back, and looked at me like a mischievous kid who had thrown a lit bottle rocket into the air, I realized he wanted me to fly the plane. *Then* I was afraid.

It all felt so foreign, so unfamiliar. Even sitting in the cockpit, wearing the fancy headphones brought no comfort. There have not been many times in my life when I've felt like I had no idea what I was doing, but in that moment I was keenly aware of my own ignorance of the art of flying. I had no experience or knowledge that would aid me in this situation.

I remember thinking, "What if he asks me to land the plane?" I didn't even get to enjoy my few moments in the cockpit because of the irrational thoughts going through my head. I tried to be logical. I was being led by a top-notch pilot who could fly without need of instruments, after all. Yet in my mind, it all boiled down to my own meager capabilities.

Similarly, we as parents experience the same feelings of disorientation and helplessness with our teens and their culture. We are afraid to address issues in their lives for fear of not knowing the right answer, or uncovering so much that we won't know what to say next. How many times have you seen something in your teen's life that gave you pause, but then you intentionally ignored it? Something in your gut said, "I might need to look into this." But no sooner did the thought come to you than you had a feeling of paralysis. A fear of not knowing the right words. A feeling that you were about to fly a plane and didn't know how.

One of my mentors (and one of the wisest men I've ever met) has been a high school principal for twenty-five years. We were talking about how difficult it is to get parents to address behavioral issues with their kids. He said, "A feeling of being unequipped or inadequate keeps parents from acting. A parent starts thinking, 'If I start tinkering with what's going on, I might push my kid away.' We put too much credence on being an expert."[4]

Our culture has developed an unhealthy dependence on and fascination with experts. Turn on cable news any time of the day, and you'll find a slew of them. Political analysts. Adolescent development experts. Personal fitness instructors. Retirement banking analysts. Urban community development experts. Anyone with a long title has immediate credibility, regardless of the usefulness or truthfulness of the advice they give. If Dr. Phil says it's so, then it's so. If Donald Trump says a stock will be hot, we buy it. In the seventies, E. F. Hutton's firm created a memorable commercial touting his ability to make us listen simply when we hear him speak.

Don't misunderstand. Experts are a good thing. Their wisdom and experience are invaluable. When our home air conditioner broke down in the heat of summer, I didn't go out and tinker with it. I called an expert: someone who could fix it quick and fix it right.

So also when it comes to raising teens, experts can be helpful. After all, you are reading this book hoping to glean a nugget or two. In our culture, a plethora of resources are at our fingertips (including Web sites, conferences, books, and school counselors). All great tools, but they are not the be-all and end-all.

At times I've thought I was not equipped to deal with my children's world. All the stories I'd heard from friends about how much they resented their own parents for things they did while raising them would start rattling around in my thoughts. I remember thinking, "If I screw this up, my daughter will hold this against me forever." Honestly, there have been times in my relationship with my children when I felt my conscience saying, "Speak truth with love." But my self-esteem said, "Shut up! If you say something wrong, you'll look stupid."

My unwillingness to help them in their culture is, in reality, an unwillingness to trust the work of the Holy Spirit in my own life. I wonder if the same might be true for you. Maybe you are like me, searching out feelings instead of seeking out the Holy Spirit. I'm learning that I may not be an expert on parenting on a daily basis, but I can trust he who is greater than the world.

Jesus said an interesting thing to his followers as they walked with him on the night he was to be betrayed and arrested. He was trying to get them to understand what would happen when he left, first dying and later returning to heaven. He said, "But the Counselor, the Holy Spirit, whom the Father will send in my name, will teach you all things and will remind you of everything I have said to you. Peace I leave with you; my peace I give you." (John 14:24–27, NIV). These people had been following

Jesus for three years. They knew more about him than anyone else. They were the founding members of his movement. But they were far from experts on his way of life. The Holy Spirit would be able to do two things for them: remind them of all they had already learned, and teach them some things that were outside of their experience. It is as if Jesus was saying, "I've only scratched the surface with you. There is so much more to be learned. There is a richer life yet ahead of you." He is taking the focus off of their capabilities, their knowledge, their experiences. Of primary importance would be what the Holy Spirit would show them, whispering to them in times of unknowing, in situations where they were not experts.

Jesus promises that you'll know when the Spirit is speaking, because you will have peace. Peace about what you are hearing. Peace about how you should respond. I know you know this peace, the voice inside you that says, "This is going to be a hard conversation for my son to have with me, but I know it's the right thing," or, "I love my daughter too much to continue to let her walk into that situation." Not that you have the words yet, but you have an assurance that your intervention is right. Having the Holy Spirit's guidance doesn't mean you have all the answers. But it does give you the ability to respond to truth when you sense it.

You don't need my permission, but I want to set you free to trust the Holy Spirit regardless of what experts say you should do. Many times at our conferences, parents will ask me questions like, "What do you think I should do about the music my son listens to?" or, "What do you think I should do about the friends my daughter is hanging out with?" My answer is always the same. It doesn't matter what I think you should do. All that matters is what the Holy Spirit is telling you to do. And I promise you he will tell you if you will listen.

The Wonder of God's Design

Walking into your teen's culture is admittedly frightening and will leave you queasy and uncertain at times, but you are not on your own. This is what God intended. Remember, he knew what he was doing when he gave you the kid(s) you have. I don't care what the circumstances were, God's matching you up with your kids was not a mistake or an accident. In fact, I want you to let these next few statements just sit with you. Ponder them. Maybe even journal out your feelings about them. Own these truths.

My children were God's intention for me.

I am part of God's plan for my children.

My children will understand God's world through me.

I can trust truth from the Holy Spirit.

Regardless of whether your journey into parenthood started as a scared teen mother, a stepparent trying to figure out complicated new relationships, or a parent by adoption—none of these circumstances changes the fact that you are a gift to your child. God not only intended for you to be a parent but saw fit that you would be his plan to help your teen understand the Creator's world. If this is his plan, then you don't have to be afraid to be a parent.

The next time you feel something in your gut saying, "Just ask what's going on," I want to encourage you to listen and engage your teenager. When you see an area of belief or behavior in your teen's life that seems out of sync with the person you know, listen and engage.

Don't give in to the thinking that says, "They'll figure this out," or "Maybe it's not that bad," or "If I just give it some time, this will work itself out." Believe that you are in your teen's life for a purpose. Believe that the Holy Spirit will lead you. Believe that you can engage your teen.

> I guess I'm learning
> What you have taught me all along
> To trust you
> Though they aren't listening
> To trust you
> Though I'm too tired to sing my song
> To trust you
>
> I guess I'm learning
> Just how much my opinion counts
> Just trust you. . . .
> I see what I need
> Is to just let go of it all
> And trust you. . . .
> Far less of me, far more of you.[5]

5

You against the World?

Jesus came not to drive the culture from the people but the sin from the culture. He came not to condemn our culture but to redeem it.

Brian McLaren[1]

— Your family is driving down the street. Your eyes (and your teens') are drawn to a billboard with a picture of an alluring woman, inviting you to "come over for free drinks."
— You're looking over your teen's sociology textbook and read a lesson on sexual development that is at odds with what you believe.
— You take your son to rent a video game and all the options he comes up with have "graphic violence, strong language, and sexual content."

Each of these are situations that any of us could face on any given day. How do you deal with such daily collisions of values? What do you do when what you have taught and modeled to your teen seems in contradiction to the world in which they live?

No matter where your teens are educated, who they hang out with, or where they go to church, there are going to be other influences around them besides you. Some are unsavory, yet still unavoidable. They are just a part of the adolescent experience. In every area of their life, at least from time to time, teens will have an influence that draws them in a direction or expresses a worldview that is contrary to truth.

Remember, we can move past the fear, blaming, isolating, or ignoring of popular culture that we discussed in the previous chapters. Many of those influences can be addressed if you are willing to live with a little messiness and discomfort. However, I'll warn you that a more faithful and effective form of parenting teens is going to require more involvement from you. Instead of becoming angry or warring against other influences, you must join in God's work to redeem them.

Engage them. (You don't have to agree with them to understand them.)

Move into them. (You don't have to be afraid of them.)

Theologically, we often think of redemption in the narrow sense of "buying back ownership." Sort of like taking soda bottles to the store and being paid to give back ownership to the store. It's easy to see this kind of redemption in what Christ did by his death. He was paying the price to "buy back" our ownership. Now we are "in him." We belong to him. But if this is all you see of Jesus's redemption, then you miss much of the beauty and complexity of his life.

For Jesus, redemption wasn't just about eternity. It was also about the everyday, the quality of a person's life right now. Jesus didn't come merely to save souls. He came to redeem his culture and bring a better life *today*.

To redeem can also mean "to convert into something of value,"[2] or "to change for the better."[3] Jesus meets a woman and frees her from the bonds of prostitution. He eats dinner with a tax collector who ends up giving back all he had stolen. These are people who have forfeited worth in their culture. He gave value to the lives of people who had lost all social standing.

With Jesus, the neglected and rejected were also redeemed. Once Jesus met a man with leprosy who believed Jesus could take away his disease. A woman suffering from bleeding for twelve years came to Jesus to be healed. In both of these situations there is no mention of eternity or "saving," yet each story is about redemption because redeeming means "helping to overcome something detrimental." Jesus provided for these people something they could not provide for themselves.

Following Christ, this is the kind of redeeming work you must do with your teen's influences. Work to improve them, change them, mold them.

Regardless of the kids, the influences in their lives are pretty consistent. Take a look at this pie chart to see the different areas of influence in a typical teen's life.[4]

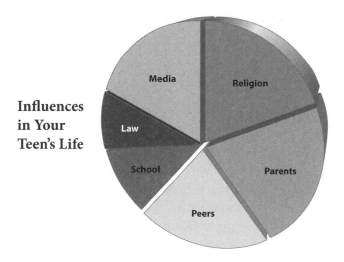

Influences in Your Teen's Life

Media · Religion · Law · School · Parents · Peers

How does it make you feel to know that you and your teen's culture are many times on a level playing field when it comes to influence? Knowing that the media can have nearly as much sway as you do is sobering. But these other areas of teens' culture will always be there. Again, your goal is not to get rid of them or to be angry at them. The goal is to be a part of them.

Think for a moment about local school. Your teens are going to spend one-third of their day in an environment in which, if you are the typical parent, you have no immediate presence or connection. But what if you volunteered a half-day each week to assist in the office or offered yourself as a teacher's assistant? Think about your gifts and abilities and how they could be used in your teen's school. If your field is computers, for instance, offer to lecture in the area of your expertise. Maybe you've always been athletically inclined and can offer to assist with one of the sports teams. Offer to chaperone the next senior trip. Perhaps offer something as small as going to your teen's teachers once a month, giving a word of appreciation, and asking if there is anything you can do. Now you've increased your presence and effectiveness in your teens' lives. Instead of you feeling at odds with the influence school may have, you are having an influence on the school.

Think about your teen's peer group. What if you offered your basement or spare room for the garage band practices? Yes, it's going to be loud, but now you are a part of it. Make your home the hangout home. When your kid brings friends over, treat them with respect. It's amazing the things your teen's friends will share with you in exchange for a fresh-baked cookie. As you embrace them, they no longer have an exclusive influence with your teen. Now you are having an influence on both your teen and his or her peers. Your overall influence is growing, and the tide is starting to turn.

As you move into these other areas of influence, remember that this is not a military coup. The goal is to redeem, not remove or conquer, cultural influences. Change will happen as you embrace your teen's peers, their school, their activities. And by love, not by force.

Oozing Pie Pieces

Breaking life down into different pie pieces makes sense to us as adults. If our lives were literally a pie, it would be fully cooked with neatly defined slices. But teens are living in a different world. Their lives don't have slices. This generation of teens has a much more organic and ever-changing approach to life. Here is what their pie of influence looks like to them.

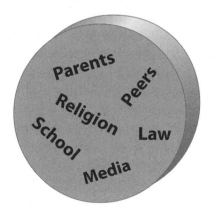

For your teens, their pie of influences has ingredients that ooze into one another. Each one has an effect on the next. It's one free-flowing pie. Each influence can easily be part of the next. In your son's mind, each one of these are easily connected and can have an impact on the other. He doesn't compartmentalize and segment life as you do. You have a work life, home life, community life, etc. Your son simply has life with all the parts flowing into the other. Perhaps this is why when one part of your son's life encounters difficulty, the whole pie can go to pieces. Each part affects the other. In his mind, you don't play a separate role in his life. You are part of the ooze of all the parts.

The only way for me not to have influence with my children's behavior and beliefs is if I willingly choose not to "ooze," to cross ingredients or categories or boundaries. If I don't talk about things that are relevant to their world, I communicate that I am not relevant to their world. If I don't talk about healthy friendships in my own life, I communicate that I don't value them. The same thing holds true when it comes to spirituality, school disciplines, extracurricular activities, or media choices.

I have a friend who works as a family counselor, helping family members reengage one another relationally. He has countless stories of teens who have fallen into areas of deep sin or depression and come to him for counseling. He has repeatedly observed parents who fail to address issues with their teens . . . and the effect that neglect has on the parent-teen relationship. He put it this way:

> Teens believe their parents know what is right and what is happening with them. When the parent doesn't talk about the teen's actions, it signals to the teen that their parent doesn't care or is possibly too ashamed of them to engage them on this level.[5]

I would add that maybe the shame isn't directed toward your teen, but at yourself. Part of God using you as a parent to redeem the influences in your teen's life could end with him redeeming your own past in the process. If you are like me, it's not hard to think of regrettable events from adolescence. There are memories of things I looked at, people I hung out with, and places I went that I wish I could erase. Even though the events were dealt with long ago, and forgiveness has been granted, there remains a voice that reminds me of my own folly of youth.

It's those areas of sin in my past that I tend to worry about the most with my own son. Issues I've wept over for the sake of my son—wishing I could take away the possibility of him revisiting experiences like those of my past. And when I'm honest, it's those very issues that I fear most when it comes to talking with my own son.

It's easy for parents to fall into the lie of believing, "I was involved in the same activity. Who am I to speak? That would be hypocritical." This is particularly true if your teen is the same age you were when you struggled with the issue. But in such cases, it's a lie that paralyzes us. Our avoidance could lead to a generational pattern that continues with our teen. I'm not speaking of "generational sin" in terms of sin being visited on your child as a punishment because of sin in your past. It's more of a pattern of behavior (or misbehavior) that, because of avoidance, gets passed down from one generation to the next. Imagine that your seven-year-old asks you if she can ride her bike around the block by herself for the first time. As you imagine her taking off, a memory from your own past races across your mind. You were seven as you trekked through the neighborhood without your parents knowing. You went block after block enjoying your two-wheeled freedom, then suddenly realized you didn't remember how to get back home. Now jump back to present-day reality. What if, because of embarrassment over your own childhood foolishness, you did nothing to prepare your own child for her trip? What might happen? She may get lost and scared, just as you did when you were a child. But because you love her and want to protect her, you don't choose avoidance. Instead, you talk or walk through the whole trip with her. Then you send her on her way. Ten minutes later, as she safely rounds the last corner for home, you celebrate her victory.

The illustration may seem simplistic, but not so much so when your daughter goes on her first date. Or your son goes to his first high school party. God has taken care of your past. Now let him use it to redeem your own teen's world. It can be painful to relive your own past, but let God use what he has done to redeem your teen's present and future. Let the words of this verse fall on you. Apply them to your past. Then live them out in your teen's present.

> So then, just as you received Christ Jesus as Lord, continue to live in him, rooted and built up in him, strengthened in the faith as you were taught, and overflowing with thankfulness. (Col. 2:6–7, NIV)

God knew what he was doing when he gave your teen to you. He has promised the Holy Spirit as counsel to you in times of uncertainty or unknowing. This doesn't mean you will speak all the right answers or always have impeccable timing. But it does mean that you will grow in the ability to know, respond, and speak the truth to your teen. There is no guaranteed outcome, but your willingness to engage their culture and be used by God to redeem the influences around them is their best chance for a healthy adolescence.

Prepared for the Next Time

So how are you going to ooze into those other influences? What effect will your life have on those areas? Begin to think through how your life can flow into other parts of your child's life. If you can find an inroad into one of these other areas, it will be much easier to flow into the next. Find the area of his life that is most accessible to you and start there.

Keep this in mind when you feel blindsided. You know it's going to happen to you, just like it does me. One day your teen is going to do or say something foolish. Or maybe you will see him or her respond to a situation in a way that is completely unhealthy. Instead of allowing yourself to hurl blame someplace else, take a deep breath and a step back. Now ask yourself a few questions:

—"How can I be more proactive?"
—"Who is someone important in my teen's life that I should talk to?"
—"What do I need to understand about this influence in my teen's life?"
—"In this situation or moment, how can I show the values of Christ to my teen?"

And perhaps the best question,

—"From now on, what can I do to be a part of that area of my teen's life?"

Now go ooze.

PART 2

ENGAGING YOUR TEEN'S HEART

6

The Writing on the Bedroom Wall

They [teenagers] are developmentally and practically preoccupied with the pleasure of the immediate because they have a driving commitment to create for themselves a world that makes life easier, safer, and more satisfying. But does that mean they have become lawless and have discarded any commitment to ethical rules and standards?

Chap Clark[1]

It was a black-and-white poster with a pink hue to it. It hung behind my door so that every night I could see her when I went to bed. She was standing in between two teenaged guys. One, slightly quirky and socially aloof; the other, the school playboy. She was torn between her affections for each of them, but in my version she would have chosen the sixteen-year-old boy that stared at her from his bed every night. She was Molly Ringwald, from the movie *Pretty in Pink*.

Molly, with her thrift-store fashion and short red hair, was the poster child for eighties alternative—a little bit of angst with a lot of individuality. To me she represented what the perfect girlfriend would be. She wasn't afraid to be herself, she didn't mind going against the norm, and she genuinely cared about her friends.

It wasn't so much what she looked like as what she represented. An ideal. And that's why I had her hanging on my bedroom door. She was the embodiment of what I valued in a girlfriend.

Before you think I'm obsessed (and I could still quote every line from that movie), this is the same reason why other guys have pictures of Budweiser girls, monster trucks, or all-star athletes. Those things represent values that are important to them. If you look below the surface, there may even be something worth championing in what it is they value so much.

You can walk into any teenager's room and get a peek into their value system just by reading the "writing" on their bedroom wall. You may see pictures of friends with handwritten captions because they value those friendships. A picture of an elite sports car with the slogan "Only the Best" can give you great insight as to how that teen views money and social status. When you see pictures of gorgeous celebrities with blurbs telling you where you can purchase what they are wearing, you can understand their values when it comes to body image and popularity. A photo of an NBA star sailing through the air with the caption "I Am What I Am" may let you glimpse your teen's deepest motivation. That bedroom is like an instant snapshot of a worldview. It's what is currently important to them. The writings and pictures may change, but the value remains the same.

The more you can understand the values of your teens, the more effective you can become at leading them. Everything they do stems from their values.

Many times, parents think teenagers make choices out of a compulsion or a total lack of reasoning. Here is a typical situation and conclusion. Your seventh-grade daughter gets in trouble at school for cheating on a test. You confront her by saying, "Why did you do this?" She responds with, "I don't know." You may conclude that she's immature and just wasn't thinking. She may or may not be immature, but don't assume she wasn't thinking.

At the time, in her mind, the choice made sense. What you don't know is that sitting next to her in class was this hunk of a guy. The Brad Pitt look-alike kind. And he was willing to pay attention to your daughter as long as she shared a few harmless answers with him while the teacher stepped out of the classroom. In her mind, the pertinent value at the moment wasn't "cheating is wrong." The motivating value was "I want to be noticed—to be important to someone." She responded out of her values. The act of cheating, in and of itself, may never even have been a factor.

Teenagers don't make decisions in a vacuum, and they think much more about their decisions than we give them credit for. A teenaged boy doesn't just wake up one morning and decide, "I'm going to get drunk today and trash my car." Neither does a girl look at herself in the mirror and conclude, "I'm going to have sex tonight and get pregnant." There were other decisions prior to these that were thought about in advance and decided on because of particular values in his or her life.

It is true that a teen's choices can appear impulsive because many times those choices are illogical or shortsighted. It would be wrong, however, to conclude teens don't think before acting. They may not process information in the same way you do, but there is still a line of thinking that can be followed.

Remember, their conclusions typically stem from a value system. Their decisions are being made because of a value they hold that may not be readily seen or evident. Even when the act itself is foolish, most of the time it is actually rooted in a value that you as a parent could affirm. Hold off on addressing the act until you find the value. Then you can help your teen determine where the thinking went wrong.

When you find out that your teen has committed an inappropriate act, how do you respond? Where is your focus? If you are like most parents (including myself many times), all your energy focuses on the act itself: Why did she do that? Didn't she know she could hurt herself? How can I keep her from doing it again?

However, placing the focus on the act and stopping there could miss the point of the act. It can also start a cycle of deceptive cover-up behavior that only makes matters worse. Sadly, if your primary goal is merely behavior modification, then what your teen takes away from the confrontation is, "Now I know what *not* to do in front of Mom or Dad."

Looking behind the Action

Even in the simplest of circumstances, it can be hard to get below the surface and see what value is being acted on. In complex matters, especially when the action is something you are morally opposed to, or a behavior that is unhealthy for your teen, the process of uncovering core values can be difficult. But it's worth the effort. And it takes a lot of practice. For example, take a look at this list of common teen behaviors:

—Sexual relationship with boyfriend/girlfriend

—Going to party where there are drugs and alcohol

—Pulling away from you as a friend; not readily opening up

—Making unhealthy media choices (movies, TV, Internet, etc.)

—Bragging about self; belittling other people.

How do these behaviors strike you? How do they make you want to respond? What would you do if your teen started doing one of these?

You would be right in wanting the behavior to stop. But you would be wrong if that was all you concentrated on. Could it be that each of these examples of unhealthy behavior, even from your own teen, could be rooted in a good value? Look at the list of behaviors again with a possible value attributed to each.

Behavior	Value
Sexual Relationship	Need for Love
Partying with Wrong Crowd	Need for Community
Distancing from Parents	Need for Purpose
Unhealthy Media Choices	Need for Authenticity
Bragging about Self/Belittling Others	Need for Self-Worth

These are values that any parent would affirm. We want our kids to have love, acceptance, and a clear purpose for living. We desire these values for our teens without remembering that they don't always know how to pursue or experience them in healthy ways. Nor do we stop to see how their inappropriate behavior could be an attempt to meet one of their God-given needs.

Recently I was talking to one of my closest friends, Brian, about this principle. He said it has completely changed the way he sees people and has greatly helped him in leading his own teenagers. For example, he said, one evening his daughter was telling him about a girl at her high school who is a lesbian. His daughter was confused and conflicted about the girl's lifestyle choice. "I just don't understand why she would want to do that," said his daughter. Brian thought about it. He tried to think about what this girl needed and how Christ loved her. He responded with, "Do you think maybe she's just desperate to be loved? Do you think maybe she thinks this is the only safe love she can find? How do you think Christ would want you to show her real love?" I was amazed. This wasn't a time for Brian to get into a discussion about the "depravity of man" or the ramifications of a homosexual lifestyle. It was an opportunity to lead his daughter in embracing others and loving them as if they are Christ.[2]

This is not to say that every time your teen is involved in unhealthy behavior there is necessarily "goodness" at the root of it. Certainly there are times we all act out of blatant disregard for what is right or good for us. We are all selfish and want our own ways. But you can begin to ask the right questions to see what is really happening, especially with your teenagers. Instead of asking yourself, "Why did she do this?" a much better question is, "What is it that she believes [value] that led her to conclude this was okay behavior [action]?" There are two different processes you can go through in a typical situation with your teen to evaluate their actions. One is behavior-oriented, and the other value-oriented. Take a look at the first example.

Behavior (action) Oriented Process

Action Committed	→	Action Addressed	→	Change in Behavior with Authority, but No Change in Values

It's easy to see where this process is going to take you. Your teen quickly learns what to do and say in front of you to keep you happy. As long as their behavior matches up with what you consider "good," they know they will have smooth relational waters with you. As a young teen, I can remember quickly learning what subjects not to broach with my parents. Politics, alcohol, partying, and even my own religious questions were off-limits for fear of making waves. I thought that as long as I was a "good kid" around them, I would be trusted and given privileges. Being honest about what I believed (and how I acted away from them) would have caused too much tension.

Maybe this is why 75 percent of all Christian teens abandon their faith when they go to college. Perhaps for them Christianity was never a core belief system, but rather a method of behavior control. So many of our Christian-based faith communities spend their energy trying to convince students of truth intellectually or to emotionally guilt-trip them into godly behavior. I've known countless youth groups, week after week, who hear messages condemning the behavior of the teens without offering a forum for teens to think through the foundation of their beliefs.

Take the issue of sex, for instance. We would all agree that sex outside marriage is not part of God's design. However, instead of answering the "why" question for students, we skip right to "because":

—Because you'll get a disease.
—Because you'll get pregnant.
—Because you'll feel guilty.

We sound just like Ralphie's mother from *A Christmas Story*. She won't let her son have a Red Ryder BB gun "because you'll shoot your eye out."

It's not that all those reasons for not having sex aren't true. They are possible consequences. But they fall short of the big picture, because they don't address or satisfy a value. They are simply external props for decreasing bad behavior.

I was talking with a church counselor about this, and he replied, "As a parent, it's just really hard to admit that when we strip everything back, what we're concerned most about is image management. We worry about how our teen's bad behavior is going to reflect on us as parents. So we just try to fix the behavior. Make it fit with an image of the accepted norm."[3]

What if instead of placing the focus on the behavior, you dealt with their value system at the core? I mentioned that there was a second way of processing decisions with your teen. Look at it this way.

Values (beliefs) Oriented Process		
Action Committed ➡️	Value in Action Addressed ➡️	Change in Behavior to Better Live Out Values

In this model, the focus is placed on the value system of your teen. If their behavior is a manifestation of what they believe, then you can affect how they behave by championing what they believe and exploring ways to achieve fulfillment of those values in healthy ways.

This process moves past conformity to what we might call "transformity." The first process says, "Do what is right." The second process says, "Be what is right." The belief has to come first, then healthy behavior can follow.

The apostle Paul said, "Do not *conform* any longer to the pattern of this world, but be *transformed* by the renewing of your mind" (Rom. 12:2, NIV). When we conform to a particular behavior, in this case that of the world, there is no foundation of belief. It's simply acting in a way that seems to be pragmatic. The world's actions give us what we want right now. You can easily see this in teens' behavior. Their behavior may be wrong, but to them it makes sense in the immediate situation.

Actually, this kind of conformity can occur with any type of behavior, whether good or bad. Furthermore, conformity may change based on the situation, creating a dualistic approach to morality. For instance, your teen may go drink with friends on Friday to avoid being rejected by friends, and then go to church with you on Sunday because it makes family life go smoothly. In his mind, neither of these behaviors contradicts the other, because in both situations the behavior achieved the desired feeling or met a need in the moment.

Transformity is altogether different. Paul says that this process occurs through a "renewing of your mind." A renewal happens over a period of time—by questioning, wrestling with, and probing the accepted behaviors of society, and then ultimately embracing God's design for what is best. In order for the conformity-based behavior to stop, an inner transformation must take place.

Perhaps this is Jesus's point when he says, "If you love me, obey my commandments" (John 14:15). He isn't interested in followers who simply obey out of duty or responsibility. Jesus tells his followers that things are going to get difficult pretty quickly. He's going to die and come back to life, then leave them and come back again sometime in the undisclosed future. That's a lot for these former businessmen and fishermen to process all in one sitting. In the same passage, he tells them the Holy Spirit will be left with them as a guide. He will instruct them. Then he speaks his famous words about love and obedience.

It's as if Jesus is saying, "If you are just along for the ride or for recognition, you won't be able to stick it out. It's going to be hard for you to obey me when the pressure comes. Then the only way you'll be able to obey my commands is if obedience is rooted in your love for me." Jesus is calling them (and us) into transformation at the core. A change in values. To love as he loves.

This is the road we must go down with our teens as well. One that leads them into a transformation of belief. One that takes into account the values of Christ.

Getting to the Core

I mentioned at the beginning of the chapter that your teen's room is a reflection of your teen's values. But what if you could peel back the pictures and posters to see what is really there? Now it's time to look more closely at what those values might be.

There are at least four core values common among teens. They are values, I would propose, that have been placed deeply within them by God. These values are intended to be genuinely met in fulfilling and appropriate ways in their lives. They can't ignore them or go without them. I'm going to go over each of the values. However, you'll need more than my help to apply what you learn in your teen's life.

Just as Jesus promised his followers the Holy Spirit would guide them into all truth, he is able to guide you in your particular circumstances as well. It is up to you to ask him to help you know how to live out these values with your teen. Ask him to show you specific ways to model each value. Ask him to show you how to lead your teen in living these values. I urge you to take some time to wrestle with these. Don't skim past them too quickly.

Value #1—Authenticity

Teens are looking for someone to be real with them. To be honest with them. To be transparent with them. One of the greatest lessons I learned from Peter Scazzero's book *The Emotionally Healthy Church* is that God does not necessarily desire for me to be a perfect person. Just a real one.[4] This is what your teens need from you, too. You don't have to have all the right answers or have everything figured out. You just need to be willing to live out the transformation process in front of them. No hiding. No faking. Hypocrisy stands out like a red flag to a teen. The only way they will learn how to be authentic themselves is if they see the real you first.

Unfortunately, realness without redemption leads to emptiness and fatalism. As teens face their own brokenness, they need healthy adults in their lives to bring truth into the experience. To point them where they need to go from where they are now.

First, then, it's up to you to be authentic in the way you talk about moral issues with your teens. Let them see, on an appropriate level, your own struggles with a moral choice. Chances are, they probably already know, but don't really want to talk openly about a subject that could divide them from you. It will be up to you to make it okay to be honest.

Second, if your teens begin to be real with you in response, they will need to know two things. One, they will not be punished for what they think or communicate to you. Two, you will still receive them even if you disagree with what they share. When you do this, you are modeling for them how to walk in repentance, forgiveness, and self-discipline in order to live a life of wholeness.

For instance, let's say your son gets up enough courage to admit to you he's fallen into a habit of consuming pornography.

And you respond with disbelief and shame. Right then you will have lost the privilege of his continued honesty in the future. It won't be worth it to him.

Of course, this doesn't mean you don't address and discipline wrong behavior, or fail to hold your kid accountable for future habits. However, the moment of vulnerability isn't the time for that. Giving your teen the freedom to divulge a moral failure eye-to-eye with a trustworthy adult is a huge step toward meeting the need for authenticity.

Value #2—Security

Maybe your daughter says things like "You don't trust me" when you don't let her go out with an older guy. Or perhaps your son says, "I'm the only one who won't be there," when you won't let him go to the after-game party. Instead of reacting defensively, listen for the unspoken value behind the spoken words. What is it he or she really wants?

No matter how grown up, every teenager wants to be protected. This may seem counter to what you hear from your teen. But at the heart of a teen is a person who longs for the security that comes from being protected from unhealthy choices and environments. I've known countless teens who were perpetually resentful toward their parents because of the carte blanche freedom they had to make their own choices. The so-called freedom led only to a lack of security and fear of making a poor choice in a situation they were not ready to handle.

In his piercing book *Hurt*, Chap Clark concludes that this is the generation of adolescent abandonment.[5] He suggests that teens today live in a world where, for most of them, Mom and Dad are so distracted by their own personal issues of pain and survival that they are unable to deal with their kids. Coaches are more concerned with creating a winning program than the character of their players. Teachers are strapped for time and resources and have little left to give to their students. All this leads to a daily fear in teens that they are truly alone to fend for themselves.

They know they are going to screw up and will disappoint you with their decisions at times. But instinctively they hide from you out of a fear of rejection or abandonment. They end up trying to figure out how to handle sin, brokenness, and pain on their own, for fear of not being received.

They want to know that you are still going to be there for them regardless of what mistakes they make. In this climate especially, your teen needs to hear these kind of words from you on a regular basis:

> "No matter what happens to you, I'm not going to abandon you."
>
> "I may not always understand you, but I'll always be here for you."
>
> "Whatever you are facing, I've got your back. I'm in your corner."
>
> "We may not always agree, but I have your best interest at heart."

Value #3—Community

In light of their impending sense of abandonment and their apprehensions about approaching adulthood, teens are looking for a place to belong. They are looking for a place where they fit, for a way to be part of something bigger than themselves. This could be one of the reasons teens far exceed adults in community-service hours. Giving to an organization builds their self-worth, but more importantly, it allows them to feel they are a part of something great.

Teens also want to be understood and feel that they have been heard by others. They look for people who receive them and validate their experience. Whether or not the people they hang out with are emotionally or spiritually healthy is of little concern once they feel part of the group. The emotional connection of community has occurred. For better or worse, it's a bond that is not easily broken. (I'm sure you can think of unhealthy friendships during your own teen years that you were not willing to lose.)

A need for community lies behind the popularity of online social networking sites such as MySpace, Facebook, and myYearbook. On these sites teens are able to post information about their lives in the form of photos, favorites, a diary, and messages to and from others. The sites are not just places for self-expression. They are places for validation. MySpace has become the most popular Web site viewed by teens on a daily basis. And for many, it is their primary outlet for community—they spend more time talking to friends online than they do in person.

Contrary to many parents' perceptions, most teenagers don't have a large group of friends. Chances are your kid is just trying to find one person he or she can confide in and be real with. It is likely that your teen will experience periods of relational drought, when there is simply not the possibility of a healthy peer community. This can be an especially sensitive time for teens, when they will especially need your support. You'll also need to fight the temptation to try and force community on them. They are looking for a place to belong, and God wants them to have it. Sometimes it just takes time to find it—sometimes, a lot of time.

For those of us who are children of the eighties, community can be difficult to embrace. We are so accustomed to being a part of a generation that valued individuality. We found our worth in our personal attainment at any cost. We largely abandoned our responsibility to creation and to one another in an attempt to make a name for ourselves. Life came down to what a person could do to make a name for himself. There was little time left for anything else and in the process we became like little islands until ourselves. Historians have labeled us the "Me Generation." Our children see the relational vacuum our lifestyle left us with, and they long for something more significant.

Your teen will let you play a role in their need for community, but it's up to you to take the first step. How can you support their activities or abilities? When your teen goes through a season of isolation or loss of friendships, how can you let them know you will walk with them through that time? What can you do to introduce them to meaningful relationships? Take some time to consider some possibilities of how you can provide community in their life.

Most importantly, the better your relationship is with your teen, the more influence you can provide in their being willing to pursue or wait for quality friendships. According to a recent study, when teens and parents have a good relationship, they tend to have friends who are less likely to fight or be delinquent. They are also more likely to be involved in extracurricular activities at school, have higher grade point averages, and have plans for college.[6]

Value #4—Affirmation

The other three values could be wrapped up and combined in the single value of affirmation. This seems to be Jesus's point when he was questioned by the religious leaders of his day. They wanted to know which commandment Jesus would say was the greatest. Jesus responded with, "'You must love the

LORD your God with all your heart, all your soul, and all your mind.' This is the first and greatest commandment. A second is equally important: 'Love your neighbor as yourself.' The entire law and all the demands of the prophets are based on these two commandments" (Matt. 22:37–40). His greatest directive correlates to man's greatest need. When your teen's need for love goes unfulfilled, everything else will begin to spiral. Author James Garbarino says, "Nothing seems to threaten the human spirit more than rejection, brutalization, and lack of love."[7]

All teenagers need to know they are valued. They need to hear it and see it on a daily basis. Just as a car tank has to be filled with fuel in order to operate, people too have "tanks." And if the size of your love-tank as an adult is comparable to that of a Volkswagen Beetle, then your teen's would be that of a gas-guzzling SUV. You might be able to go a few days without being refilled (affirmed), but your teen cannot. He or she needs refilling every day.

God has created your teen to be loved in specific ways. And if you have multiple children, those ways may be different. Become a student of your teens. Try showing them love in different ways and see what happens. If one of your attempts doesn't seem to register with them, try it a different way. Maybe they don't need more time with you, but more words. If not your words, then your touch. No matter how many ways or times you try, none is in vain. Any attempt to love your teens is noticed by them, even if they don't respond the way you had hoped.[8]

Remember that all your teens' needs come down to their overarching need to be loved by you. When you show them the real you and allow them to be authentic, they will know they are loved. When you alleviate fear by showing acceptance, they will feel loved by you. And when you provide a place of belonging and an environment for quality relationships, they'll know it is because of your deep love and affirmation of them.

Two Hands, One Hand, No Hands

The first place your teen looks to have these four values actualized is in the context of his or her relationship with you. I realize this may not seem to match up with your experience, but several recent studies have shown that the first person teens *want* to come to for advice is their parents. This shouldn't surprise us, since this is exactly as God designed it. But in reality, very few teens actually come to a parent first. Unfortunately, none of the studies have attempted to pinpoint the breakdown between a teen's desire for parental help and their ultimate unwillingness to seek it out.

Most teens have little idea how to have their values met. They end up wandering aimlessly, trying to find their way. And many times we parents have done a poor job of pointing them in the right direction. Think of their values like the finish line in a race. We lined them up on the starting line. We coached them through some of the motions of running. We even told them the objectives. These are all good things. But many teens would say that once the starting gun fired, we walked away and left them to figure out how to run the race on their own.

They really don't want to figure out life by themselves. They don't want you to leave them alone. And to leave them on their own is to set them up for a moral failure. Writer Patricia Hersch said, "The more we leave kids alone, don't engage, the more they circle around on the same adolescent logic that has caused dangerous situations to escalate."[9] When you leave them on their own, they not only continue in the same pattern of unhealthy behavior, but it typically gets worse. They want your hands-on attention.

Do you remember when your child was about a year old and decided his crawling days were over? He was ready to walk! I know it was a long time ago, but can you remember what your role was in teaching him to walk? Stop for a moment and get the mental picture. Where were you? What did you do?

I'm pretty sure you didn't stand him up in the middle of your living room, take your hands off, and say, "Now go for it!" Chances are you stood behind him, held both of his hands, and helped him take those first few awkward steps. After days of this same routine, repeated over and over, you started walking next to him, holding on to one of his hands. Finally, the day came that you knelt down on the other side of the living room, looked at your little one, and said, "Okay, come to me. Walk to me. Just take some steps."

The process you went through to teach your child to walk is the same process for teaching your teen to walk through life and live out his values. You are someone who has the wisdom of life experiences. Your teen is looking for you to be out in front of him, showing the way, drawing attention to danger ahead, helping him navigate the tight turns. You may potentially be the only one in his life standing in the distance beckoning to him, "This is the way to healthy relationships and wise choices. Follow this path!" He is willing to follow, if you are willing to show the way.

If his values and needs are not being fulfilled by you, then he will go elsewhere to find someone who can meet them. There have been many times when my daughter is sitting with me that I find myself thinking that if I don't love her the way she needs to be loved by her father, then she'll go try to find love someplace else. I've noticed with my son that as long as I'm showing him attention, in that moment, he doesn't seem to need it from anyone else. I'm giving him what he needs for today. I've been given a once-in-a-lifetime chance to model the values that Christ has innately placed in my children. You've been given the same privilege with your children.

The only hope I have of being able to meet their needs is if my own needs have first been met in Christ. I can love my daughter like a father should only if I have first been loved by my heavenly Father. There are days when I find myself not believing that I am who God says I am, and days when I think I'm not loved by him at all. Those are the days I feel I have nothing to offer the ones entrusted to me. When I become preoccupied with feelings of "me" and looking out only or especially for me, then my family feels like a distraction more than a gift. I'm not able to give, because I haven't received.

God has chosen me as a vessel to show his love to my kids, even if I am merely a "jar of clay." Ultimately, I don't want my children to look to me for their fulfillment. My life, even years into this journey with God, is still fragile. Every time I interact with others, I'm reminded of my relational inadequacies. Being still and quiet is difficult, because it's then that I'm reminded of my past and how deeply flawed I am. My selfishness and sin mock me. There are some days I can barely think of the right choices to make for myself, much less for my family. Because of his good grace, our Creator wraps his hands around this vessel of who I am and holds the crumbly pieces together to use me in my family. But in those moments when I take my relationship with my kids into my own hands—trying to be Super Dad who does no wrong, is all-knowing, and has a boundless reservoir of love—then I fail.

Miserably.

And so will you.

It was never God's design for you to be the be-all and end-all source of life for your kid. God is. You are simply the first conduit he uses to reach them. He'll also use schoolteachers, friends, youth pastors, relatives, coaches, or camp counselors. But his first choice is to use you. Isn't that amazing?!

The only way you and I can be a reflection of God to our teens is to be surrendered to him. Take some time for yourself today to hear God's voice. Let him see your jar of clay for what it is. Don't be afraid of the flaws. Don't cover the scars. Let God fill you with his love, his spirit, his wisdom, his energy. Let him give you today what you need for your teenager. Ask him what he desires for your teen and how he wants to use you today in your teen's life.

7

You Will If It Kills Me

No matter how calmly you try to referee, parenting will eventually produce bizarre behavior, and I'm not talking about the kids. Their behavior is always normal.

Bill Cosby[1]

The key to successful leadership is influence, not authority.

Ken Blanchard[2]

A clock started the moment your child was born. A countdown began. And the older they get, the louder you hear it.

Tick. Tick. Tick.

You don't know what it is or why you keep hearing it. But one day it goes off. And the shrill clang of the hammer hitting those tiny bells is both annoying and frightening. It's like being startled from a restful daydream.

What could possibly be so startling? It happens the day you talk to your twelve-year-old about a moral issue and they say, "I don't believe that anymore," or "That might work for you, Dad, but it doesn't work for me." Or maybe it was when your fifth-grader said, "Mom, please don't hug me when you drop me off. Some of the guys are standing outside," or "Dad, when my friends get to the house, would you just give us some space?"

In your own mind, nothing changed between the two of you. Everything was going fine. But for your eleven- or twelve-year-old "tweenager," their universe will never be the same again. Neither will yours. In a matter of what seemed like a moment's time, a shift in influence took place. In reality the shift was taking place over many months, but you either didn't see it or couldn't acknowledge it.

I've experienced this same uncomfortable shift with my son. On a visit to Blockbuster, he found an action film that he wanted to rent. It was one of those historical films about pilots and war. Guy stuff. I thought it might be fun watching it together, so I said we could get it but that I'd have to watch it first to make sure that it wasn't too graphic. That night while I watched the film, he came into my room twice to "ask a question," which translated into "I'm dying to see it, and have got to catch a peek." I said I thought it looked safe enough, but he would have to wait until the next night when we could watch it together.

The next morning he came into our home office. "Dad, I can't wait to see *Flyboys*. It looks so cool." Two hours later he came back. "So do you think we can start the movie right after supper?" And just for good measure, he came back again an hour later. "Can I watch the whole thing or do we have to skip some of it? 'Cause if there's any blood and guts, I don't have to see that. I just want to see them flying the planes."

Right before supper he asked if I would go out back and pitch some baseballs to him. I love those moments more than anything we do together, so of course I said yes. But as we headed outside, a friend of his from down the street came to ask if he could join us. I am man enough to admit that I didn't want him to come. It was our moment. Just father and son. But through my jealous thoughts I ignored the faint sound of the ticking clock.

We stayed outside until time to eat. As we were packing up the bat and balls, Bailey's friend said, "Hey, Bailey, you wanna come over after you eat?" Excited at the invitation, Bailey responded, "That'd be great. Can I go, Dad?"

Now I was thinking to myself, "No, he can't because he's going to be watching a movie with me." I tried a gentle reminder. "If we don't start that movie as soon as dinner is over, then we won't get to see it before bedtime." I thought it would be an easy choice. He had looked forward to our time together all day.

Tick. Tick. Tick.

"But, Dad, I would rather go to my friend's house than watch the movie with you."

What? During my son's whole life up to now, I have been the "it" guy. The guy he did everything with. I wasn't an afterthought or a plan B. I was the first person on his list. But in that awkward moment, a moment where I felt defensive and insignificant, I knew that his world was no longer just about me.

There was a shift in influence taking place in his life. And the way I responded to it would largely determine how much weight I'd get to carry in his decision making for the rest of his teen years. The same is true with you and your teen (or preteen).

The Way the Universe Spins

Maybe you're wondering what this has to do with influence. Isn't all this just part of a child's growing up? Isn't it a natural thing? The answer to these questions is both yes and no. Yes, it's natural for your teen to have other influences and interests in his or her life. But no, it's not natural for you to lose influence. The types of influence you have will always be changing, but your influence should always be present.

Think of yourself and your child as parts of your own solar system. When your child was small, the solar system looked like this.

Authoritative Influence

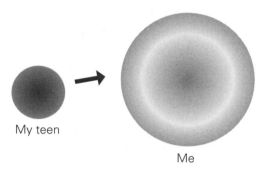

My teen

Me

You were the center of your child's world. You were the strongest pull. Just as the sun keeps the planets in order, you kept your child's world in order. You were it. Whatever you said went. For the most part, regardless of the answers you gave, your child believed them and acted on them. When your little boy asked you where his goldfish went when it died, and you said "Heaven," he believed it, because that's what you said. When your little girl asked when she could wear a shirt that shows her belly button like Lindsay Lohan, and you said "Never," she shrugged her shoulders and said okay, because you were the moral and social center of her universe.

But something happens between the ages of ten and thirteen. A child's universe changes. Now it looks like this.

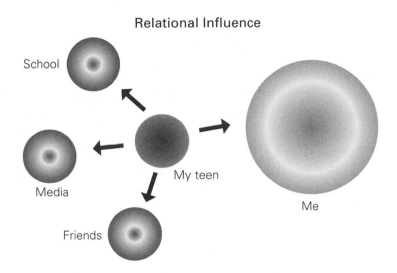

Relational Influence

Now there are many forces—major influences—at play. And it's not so much that your influence doesn't have pull. It's more that the sum of other influences working together in your teen's new universe have a weightier effect. Together they produce a greater gravitational pull. These influences appeal to a different part of life that has newly awakened—relationships. Specifically, relationships apart from you. And no matter who the teen is, in this new universe, peer relational influence always trumps authoritative influence.

Look at it this way. How many employees at your workplace naturally hang out at the boss's house on the weekend? It just doesn't happen. The boss isn't your buddy. He or she is the person who tells you what to do or not do, and then rewards you for your performance. The boss's influence in your life is purely authoritative. A real relationship with him or her is rarely a factor.

Many teens see their parents this way. Parents are there to remove all the fun and spontaneity from life. They dictate what can or can't be done. They don't relate. They simply try to control.

I'm sure you would agree that there is a problem with this perception. I've never met parents who would describe their role as being their teen's employer. Who doesn't want their teen to experience a full, exciting life? Most parents' goal is to lead their teen, not control them. A power play is not your heart's intent.

The problem for most parents is navigating through the transition. It is extremely difficult to go from being an authoritative influence, where you are the main force, to a more relational influence, where there are many other forces vying for your teen's attention. But if parents don't make the shift to include both types of influence within their teen's life, then everyone loses and the relational gulf between parent and teen widens.

As other forces in your teen's universe pull on him, he starts spending more and more time with these new friends. His interests change and he wants to spend hours playing Xbox with these friends instead of playing baseball with you. He comes to you less and less for advice because now he gets a wealth of advice from his buddies at school and the neighborhood, not to mention all his Facebook "friends." He comes home from school and asks you if he can spend the night with one of his new friends. Now you've never met this kid, but you've heard some things from other parents about his home life and you have a strong feeling that this is not a good idea. As a matter of fact, your mind is made up before he's even finished explaining why he has to be allowed to go.

Without even thinking, words start coming out. "Absolutely not. That's just not possible. I've never met his parents. I don't even know anything about this kid. What do you even know about him?"

Your son says, "I know he's my friend. I know he wants to hang out with me. And I know I don't want to be home another Friday night!"

Sarcastically you respond with, "Oh I know. Things are so hard for you at home, aren't they? Life is just miserable in our home. Besides I didn't say you couldn't go out on Friday night. I just said there's no way you're spending the night with that new . . . *friend* of yours."

"Why do you say it that way? Why do you judge all my friends like they're bad people or something? Does that make me a bad person 'cause I like to hang out with them?"

The last sound you hear is the door slamming as he storms out of the room. And nothing was really accomplished. Sure he knows he can't go to the friend's house, but that was never the point of the conversation. Again, when you attempt to solely use your authority to control your teen, then everyone loses.

As your teen's universe continues to grow, it's easy to feel a loss of control and, if you're honest, maybe even some jealousy towards those other influences. But the goal isn't to reassert control or your dominance over his world. Instead you want to teach healthy choices and help prepare him for the time when you are not around. This requires a balance of both authority and relationship.

Internalizing this concept will take some honesty on your part. Take a moment and think about a recent conflict with your teen. Maybe the one from yesterday. What was it about? Why did you disagree? Was there a line drawn in the sand over the issue? What set you off?

Now I want you to look at a few questions about your con-flicts and give an honest answer to yourself. Remember that you are not the only one who already knows the answers to these questions. Your teen does too.

Question 1
Did I hear . . .
 a) the facts of the situation?
 b) the heart of my teen?
 c) both the facts and my teen's heart?

Question 2
Was I preoccupied with . . .
 a) changing my teen's behavior?
 b) understanding my teen's values?
 c) both?

Question 3
As we talked did I . . .
 a) try to control my teen's choice?
 b) try to guide my teen's choice?

Question 4
In the end, was I . . .
 a) doing damage control?
 b) leading them through a transformation?

If you honestly answered "a" to a number of these questions, I want you to know I'm right there with you. It's so much easier for me to be the authority and to just say no than it is to take the time to really listen, use discernment, and respond in a way that leaves my son feeling that he has a clear grasp on what is best and healthy for him. Let's pause to explore some dynamics that seem especially to affect fathers.

The Empty Dad Syndrome

The transition from authoritative to relational influencer seems particularly difficult for dads. Something about including in the equation both the facts and the heart in situations can be problematic for men. To be both authoritative and relational takes a great amount of energy and focus. And energy and focus are two things most overworked, Western-culture parents have little of when they get home each evening.

If you are a working dad (or working mom), see if this picture fits your life. You spent all day making critical decisions about a job project. You focused your attention on the company's or customer's needs. You poured all your energy into doing a good job. Then, after being on the clock for nine or ten hours, as you are leaving, you get a call that keeps you there another forty-five minutes. You finally walk in the door of your home, exhausted. Now you're expected to give the same amount of attention, focus, and energy to your family for the next three hours. And we both know (actually everyone in your home knows), it's just not possible.

According to one study, 64 percent of teens spend an average of 4.5 minutes a day in conversation with their dads.[3] One could argue that you can neither be an authority nor have a relationship in four and a half minutes a day. This almost-absentee dad shows up for a few minutes to make sure the rules are still being kept and that there is some semblance of order. There is just not enough time left to invest in being the kind of influence that is most critical to a teen's well-being.

There is also evidence to support that the longer a dad goes without being a relational influence, the more distant his teen will become. I worked on a team that conducted a study involving high schoolers and their beliefs and behaviors. We asked the students to affirm the truthfulness of the statement, "I have a close relationship with my mother." The same statement was then posed of the father. Take a look at the obvious differences in the two graphs.

With moms there is a slight natural fluctuation from year to year, but there is an overall consistency. But with the dads, there are no fluctuations; it's a decline every year, with the largest drop happening between ninth and tenth grade. If you are a dad, here's another hard question for you: what would your own teen's chart look like in response to the statement in the survey?

I have a close relationship with my mother.

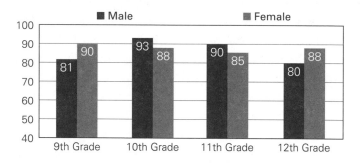

I have a close relationship with my father.

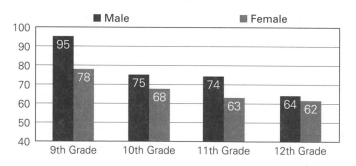

The sentiments of these teens are echoed nationwide. In every relational category with teens, fathers lag behind mothers. Teens are more likely to do something special with and seek advice from their mothers. They also feel loved more often by their mother as well as take more pride in and show more love to them.[4]

One with the Other

If you are like me, and the possibility of this kind of reality fills you with fear and worry, then there is hope. It doesn't have to be this way. Just because 36 percent of high school senior guys have a distant relationship with their dads, that doesn't mean it has to be so in your case. It is possible for you to be both authoritative and relational with your teen.

Chances are you are doing better at one type of influence than the other. It could be because it's what comes naturally to you and feels comfortable. Maybe it's your default under pressure. But now you've got to begin to think through ways to be the other type of influence. You can do what wasn't modeled for you or doesn't naturally flow from you. You need a healthy balance of both influences.

As your teen gets older, the only way you can continue to be an authoritative influence is by choosing to be a relational influence as well. Teens need you to both speak the truth and listen to their opinion. They need you to require moral boundaries as well as love them through their moral failures. They need you to point them in the right direction and walk with them to their destination. All of your rules, directions, and guidelines will translate into positive life change on your teens' part only if they see and receive how you love them.

The tension between you and all those influences in your teen's world can seem almost maddening at times. Be encouraged that this is probably a temporary change. In most cases the world of influence in a teenager's life ends up just as God designed it, with the parents being the strongest influence. For most teenagers the strongest pull away from their parents is in middle school. There have been many studies over the years that have all come to the same conclusion—in the end parents far outweigh any other influence. Chap Clark says that parents are by far the weightiest long-term influence in a teenager's life, with peers having the most short-term influence, particularly during middle adolescence. Media culture has an impact on views of self and immediate feelings, but its influence is fleeting compared to what you have as a parent.[5]

Christian Smith, with the National Study of Youth and Religion, recently conducted the most exhaustive study concerning teenagers' beliefs and behaviors in spirituality. Smith said, "For better or worse, most parents in fact still do profoundly influence their adolescents—often more than do their peers—their children's apparent resistance and lack of appreciation notwithstanding."[6] It may not look like it, it may not feel like it, but your teen is being impacted by you.

Another observation of the study was that most parents do not realize how much of an impact they have on their teen's spiritual beliefs. Of parents who said their faith was extremely important to their daily life, 67 percent of their teens reported the same conviction. Of those parents who said faith was somewhat important in daily life, 61 percent of their teens said the same thing. Smith noted that "the most important social influence in shaping young people's religious lives is the religious life modeled and taught to them by their parents."[7]

When you are in the thick of the teen years, you may feel a tearing away; you may feel an aggression and a resistance from your teens. But regardless of how difficult the relationship becomes, they still are learning from you.

When All Is Broken . . . but God

All this talk of influence can be particularly hard for a parent whose relationship with his or her teen has been altered by a divorce. If you live apart from your teen, the few minutes' contact a day ends up happening on the phone. And even the single parent with custody is usually so busy just trying to keep things afloat that there is little time left for nurturing. A twenty-five year study of divorce has shown that ten years after the breakup only one-quarter of fathers and one-half of mothers were able to provide the kind of nurturing relationship for their children that they had before the divorce. The distance between parent and teen causes a loss of both authoritative and relational influence that many times is difficult to repair. Author Judith Wallerstein says, "At the threshold of young adulthood, relationships move center stage. But for many that stage is barren of good memories for how an adult man and woman can live together in a loving relationship."[8]

If you are in this situation, as a mom or dad, my heart hurts for both you and your teen. I don't pretend to know the hurt and loss you feel with your teen in trying to maintain a growing relationship. And I pray these few words do not come across as trite. Thinking about all that has happened can be painful and bring up unhappy memories, but God can redeem your relationship with your teen. Whether divorced, remarried, widowed, or hanging by a thread, when things are going wrong the greatest hope you have is in two simple words . . . "but God."

But God cares. But God listens. But God heals. But God redeems. But God weeps. But God soothes. But God whispers. But God laughs.

8

A Passionate Story

Those who danced were thought to be quite insane by those that could not hear the music.

Angela Monet[1]

It wells up inside of me whenever I watch movies like *Braveheart*, *Remember the Titans*, or *Saving Private Ryan*. There is this undefinable urge, an almost unexplainable need to do something, to make a difference.

There is a particularly intense scene in *Braveheart* where the DVD player seems to ooze testosterone. William Wallace, covered in war paint and sweat, is standing before thousands of his countrymen. The fear in their eyes is obvious as they look across the battlefield at the countless numbers of their enemy. On horseback, Wallace rides back and forth like an angry lion as he shouts these words: "Fight, and you may die. Run, and

107

you'll live . . . at least awhile. And dying in your beds many years from now, would you be willing to trade all the days from this day to that for one chance, just one chance, to come back here and tell our enemies that they may take our lives . . . but they'll never take our freedom!"[2] With swords thrust in the air, his men respond with shouts. And something inside me says, "Get up. Do something! Make a difference!"

I remember going to the movies in seventh grade with my best friend Wayne to see *Rocky III* for the fifth time. We stood at the back of the long, dark theater waiting for the familiar music. To this day, no matter where I am when those trumpets begin to blare, I respond by jogging in place and throwing jabs at my invisible foe. And when the music came on that day in the crowded movie theater, we came running down the aisle. We thought we were the epitome of cool. And don't pretend you didn't do something just like it. I know you did.

There is something inside every one of us, including your teenager, that says, "Do something." We can't help it. We know, deep down in our gut, that there is more to life than mere existence. We want to give ourselves to something or be a part of something greater than ourselves.

That urge—that push for more—*that* is passion. Joss Whedon said, "Passion lies in all of us, sleeping . . . waiting. It speaks to us . . . it guides us. Passion is the source of our finest moments. The joy of love, the clarity of hatred, and the ecstasy of grief. It hurts sometimes more than we can bear. Without passion we'd be truly dead."[3]

Even small children have passion. We just refer to it with other names, like imagination or daydreams. At a young age we have the ability to create in our mind a whole world full of adventure and possibilities. Could it be that all those days dancing around your living room in ballerina tights or brandishing sticks as pirate swords was the beginning of a passion being born in you? I remember as a little boy wanting to be a cowboy, then an astronaut, then Luke Skywalker. The dreams always got bigger and more fanciful. But what I really wanted was to be part of something greater than myself.

I had the opportunity to listen to author Donald Miller talk about this not long ago. He never actually used the word "passion" in his talk, but it is what he was getting at. A writer himself who weaves beautiful stories, Miller talked about our lives in terms of a story. A story we are each working on. A story we would want to be great. A story we would want everyone else to read.[4]

Stop and think about this for a moment. What kinds of stories do you like to read? Better yet, if someone wrote a screenplay of your life, what kind of story would you want it do be? An epic romance? A modern comedy? A Greek tragedy? I think mine would be a drama. The kind of multilayered drama with deep characters, a strong plot, and a great eighties soundtrack.

I remember Miller saying, "Every good story involves risk and resolution." Stories without risk are . . . well, boring. And so is life at times. We want to be part of something great. Something bigger than ourselves. Some people are even willing to die for something greater than themselves.

Your teen doesn't want to just graduate high school, go to college, get a good job, and live in a nice house in the suburbs. That was the dream of the eighties generation. A lifestyle of comfort and excess. We parents of today's teens grew up in a culture where the passion was consumerism. Each time I speak to teenagers, I see them searching for what will give their life meaning. They recognize that the mere idea of Jesus isn't enough. They want to know how to radically live for him. Real purpose will not be found in the comfort of a gated community, but in how they can expand the boundaries of God's kingdom.

They aren't looking for safe and predictable; they are looking for significance and wonder. I've never heard of a teenager coming home from a mission trip—where they were able to put their passion into action, experience a world greater than themselves, and serve alongside a team of spiritual pilgrims—and responding with, "That was okay, but Six Flags is better." Instead, I've seen countless teenagers come home ignited with passion. It fizzles only when they are not able to find the same opportunities in the daily confines of life back at home.

We must give our teens opportunities at home, in our communities, to partner with God in his story of redemption. They don't have to go half a world away to be used by God and feel that their lives have purpose. We must allow them not only to dream but to put dreaming into action, to stand on the edge of the unknown and jump into an ever-expanding story.

This can be difficult for parents, because we are conditioned to keep our children safe, to protect them at all costs. But as we attempt to protect them from harm, both physical and emotional, we risk squelching their passion. Maybe one of the reasons so many college students walk away from their faith is because we make it too reasonable and boring. Or, as Miller put it, "They simply went looking for a better story."

What a tragedy it would be if our teens walked away because the faith we showed them seemed to suck the life out of them. Many years ago Jim Rayburn, the founder of Young Life, said, "It's a sin to bore a kid with the gospel."[5] Jesus was not the predictable bore with pasty white skin we have made him out to be. He was a guy who left the protection of his mother and father, didn't know where he would lay his head at night, and trusted the God who feeds the sparrows to feed him as well. He was willing to experience this kind of personal vulnerability for the chance of seeing lives changed by love.

Just Say Yes

A few years ago one of my interns, Lauren, felt something stirring inside her. She began to be willing to put herself at risk, to make a difference. During this time she heard a missionary speak about untouched people groups in Asia. In that moment there was immediate clarity. God began to give her a growing passion for the people of Tibet. After months of studying everything she could about these amazingly resilient and tender people, she dropped the bomb on her parents: "I want to go live out the gospel with people in Tibet." She wanted to spend the next two years as a university student in Tibet, in order to form relationships with those her age that had never heard the gospel.

Lauren's dad talked to me a few days after she presented her "exciting news." Lauren's dreams, desires, passions, and even God's will were of little concern to him at that particular moment. All his thoughts were of fear for his daughter. His wife's were more along the lines of terror. As a matter of fact, her mom's first response was, "Absolutely not." But nothing could curb Lauren's passion. Knowing she would be the first (and only) female to be part of the group of university students to go to Tibet didn't change her mind. The more she prayed and dreamed, the more her passion grew.

As a sociology professor, Tony Campolo has spent much of his adult life taking college students to Haiti, where they can experience life outside suburbia. He has spent years inviting students to be a part of God's story to redeem one of the poorest countries on our planet. God has used him to stir a passion in hundreds of students for the least of these—the discarded and forgotten of society. He said that the first question many parents ask before letting their kids go is, "Will this be safe?" He responds with, "Of course it won't be safe! When did Jesus ever say living for Him would be safe? There will be many risks . . . but much reward."[6] Culture shaper Shane Claiborne said, "Family is one of the most significant barriers to potential risk-takers who would leave everything for the way of the cross."[7]

How you respond to a passion God has birthed in your teen may either set them free to experience a yet unknown depth with God, or it could create a root of resentment and confusion toward you as well as toward spiritual matters. As guardian, you still have the responsibility for discernment, and only you can answer whether you are making a decision that is in your kid's best interest or one that simply makes you feel good. But regardless of the conclusion, I can't stress enough *the importance of handling a teen's passion with seriousness.*

After speaking to a group about social justice and commitment to making a difference, a high school girl came up to me to share with me her desire to go to New York City to do summer missions. She shared her grief and hurt over telling her parents about her idea. Her parents responded with, "When God tells us that you need to go to New York, then you can go to New York." End of conversation. She felt that they dismissed her and that her passion was unimportant. Worse, she felt confused. She began to question that maybe she misheard the Holy Spirit or didn't hear him at all. Maybe she made the whole thing up in her imagination to make herself feel better emotionally. Regardless as to whether her parents felt uncomfortable or felt it was the wrong time or whatever the reason—she needed to be heard and given a thoughtful answer. Maybe something as simple as, "That is really cool, sweetie, that you want to be used by God and that you are listening for his voice. I know this sounds like it may be a good opportunity but I'm honestly not sure about it. Why don't we both agree to pray about it before I make a decision?"

It can be hard to take a teenager's passionate interest in different issues seriously at times, because it seems almost crazy. In fact, once passion is set in motion, it can look absolutely foolish on the surface. Just consider a few examples from our own spiritual heritage who acted on their passions. A young shepherd named David goes to deliver food to his brothers on the battlefront. Upon his arrival he sees his brothers, as well as the rest of the Hebrew army, cowering in fear at a giant of a man who is cursing Jehovah. The fear within the Hebrews was immobilizing them against the challenge to fight. No one dared to face Goliath. David could see the defeat in the eyes of his countrymen, but that wasn't what led him to act. It was his passion for God's honor. This young teenager, whose puberty hadn't afforded him enough body mass to fill out a soldier's armor, faced the giant with nothing more than a slingshot and a few rocks. And with God. Talk about a passion that looks foolish!

There's another testosterone-filled story from our spiritual history from one of Israel's prophets named Elijah. A wicked king named Ahab ruled over Israel. Besides leading the people to worship the false gods of Baal, part of Ahab's legacy included letting his evil wife, Jezebel, kill all of God's prophets. To top it off, there was a great famine in the country. Not a lot going well for the Israelites at this time.

Elijah, the lone remaining prophet, had had enough. He went before the king to issue a challenge. Like David, he was saddened by the state of his people. But what moved him was a passion for God's name. He single-handedly took on 450 prophets of Baal in a sort of BBQ cooking contest. Whichever god could ignite the altar would be declared the one true God. I can't help but think that if you and I were there watching this scene unfold, we would have said Elijah was insane. But he was also a man of passion following God's command.

What if your teen came home from school and said, "I want to end AIDS in Africa by shooting free throws?" This happened to the parents of Aaron Gutwein, a nine-year-old from Arizona. In school, Aaron was learning that the AIDS epidemic had orphaned 15 million children in Africa. Aaron decided to use what he did best, shooting basketball, to raise money for the orphaned children. His parents could have said, "You'll be laughed at. Don't get your hopes up." Or, "Who would give you money for playing basketball? Besides you don't know anyone with any influence." Instead they said, "Okay." The first year Aaron raised $3,000. The next year he partnered with World Vision and recruited more than a thousand friends to participate. They raised $38,000. The third year his dream spread to more kids, and they raised more than $100,000 to build a school in Zambia for orphans. It may have seemed foolish to some in the beginning, but I think there are some children in Zambia who are grateful Aaron's parents said yes.[8]

Lauren, mentioned earlier, was filled with the same foolishness. I saw her parents struggle, as any parent would, to trust God's movement in their daughter's life. But they released her to this God-given passion. I should probably also tell you that Bill and Heidi have always had a great relationship with Lauren that is a little different from some families. They have both taken an active interest in her spiritual formation. They guide her, lead her, even prod her when necessary to discover all God has in store for her. So while their initial response was to protect the daughter they love, they were not going to say no to a passion planted by God. Saying yes to God's dream in her didn't take away their fear or make it any less stressful to watch her get on a plane bound for the other side of the world. But it did mean that for the next two years they could trust God and release Lauren to write an amazing chapter in her life's story.

All Shapes and Sizes

Maybe you're reading this and thinking, "I'd be happy if my son lived for something greater than the top score on the latest Need for Speed video game." Or maybe you feel like all your daughter does is mope around the house complaining about how bored she is. There could still be a passion inside. It may be untapped. It may be undiscovered. But it's there.

Sometimes that passion is hard to identify because we tend to view passion as connected to a cause much like Lauren going to Tibet. Something you can calculate, set goals for, measure your success in. For a great many teenagers, their passions are more relational in nature. They look out for the needs of their friends. This generation, unlike my own, is exploring new ways to live in community with one another. Many of them are entering into conversations with one another about rediscovering how to live in peace together. These ideas are close to God's heart, but easily overlooked when we are drawn toward charisma rather than quietness.

When we see strong personalities in a dramatic movie, or perhaps on the platform at church, it's easy to think that those are the only kind of people God uses. In our minds, by default, those with the more extroverted qualities seem to be the most important people. When we think this way, we end up short-changing God's plan in the lives of those who don't aspire to the limelight.

First Corinthians 1:25–31 is a passage that gives me hope. It's the passage wherein Paul tells us the kind of people through whom God chooses to glorify himself: foolish, weak, lowly, despised. This gives misfits like me hope. I think part of what Paul is getting at here is that we belong to a God who stirs a passion within the most unlikely people. When Jesus encountered a broken Mary Magdalene, she was moved. Quiet servants like Martha were given verbal recognition. Andrew, a younger brother and follower by nature, is chosen as one of the Twelve. In the Old Testament, God uses a reserved and insecure man like Moses to lead his people. And Nathan, a subordinate to King David, is given a passion for justice.

Contrary to what our Wall Street culture teaches, traits like compassion, quietness, contemplation, and submission are not character flaws. These kinds of qualities in teens can be just as passionate, even when displayed in different ways. We need look no further than Mother Teresa, Gandhi, and Rosa Parks to see that kind of passion. Their passion manifested itself in nonviolent protests against injustice, in compassion for forgotten societies, and in a lifelong commitment to loving the "unlovable."

Whether extroverted or introverted, your teenagers were made by God to live a passion-filled life. Because it is his purpose to give your teens' lives purpose, one day the reservoir inside them will spill over, and you will see them move. You'd better get out of the way or get on board.

Living for Greatness

Francine Rivers has written a series of historical fiction on the founding and frailty of the early church. She spends a great many pages describing not just what the church endured, but what was happening in the Roman culture. Of that culture she says, "These conquerors of the world are slaves to their passions, and someday their passions will bring them down."[9]

It would be easy enough to conclude that the passions she refers to are both politically driven and sexual in nature. In fact, it is difficult to locate a moral compass in Roman culture when it came to sexual practices. Anything was allowed. Their gods practiced bestiality, participated in orgies, and accepted incest.

What was good enough for their gods was good enough for the people. From the picture painted by many Roman historians, their practices would make many in our entertainment culture blush.

It would be easy to stop at the surface. But I think the passion that Rivers refers to is much more insidious and rooted in the heart of us all. *It is a passion for our own greatness.* A passion for power and glory.

The downfall of the Roman Empire wasn't merely lust for sexual gratification. It was also lust for personal conquest. Each emperor had to outdo the other. Bigger statues. More powerful armies. Conquest for more land. In the end, the empire grew so big geographically that it outgrew its ability to protect itself. The emperors' greatness was literally their greatest weakness.

That same lust for greatness lives in us. It is difficult for us to see in ourselves as adults, and nearly impossible for our teens to admit. When every billboard and ad tells you that you can (and should) make yourself prettier, wealthier, and happier, it's hard not to give all you've got to make a name for yourself. The message our teens need to hear from us is that the only "greatness" that will last is God's glory.

We must lead them in such a way that they can die to their own self-centeredness and self-preservation. We have to encourage their God-given passion to be part of something greater than themselves and help ensure that the "greater thing" is his kingdom. The most intense, risky, and challenging pursuit we can lay before them is a deep passion for God's name. If we want to set our kids up for success, we must invite them into God's best—his greatness.

Louie Giglio defines passion as "what you are willing to endure to reach the prize."[10] I would add to that, "and what you are willing to give up." It's impossible for me to be part of God's greatness while making a name for myself. The apostle Paul

117

struggled with this as well. In his letter to Philippi, he longs for his friends to understand that greatness comes with death. A death to one's own desires, ambitions, and achievements.

He knows the esteem in which his friends hold him. Perhaps some even idolize him. Maybe he sees that they put him on an superhuman pedestal, as we too easily do with many of our pastors today. I can see the same conversations happening back then that we have today. One person asks, "So where is your family worshipping these days?" "We are at First Church of Philippi, right past the marketplace." The conversation follows, "Oh, I've heard a lot of folks talking about it. Who's the pastor over there?" Then comes the praise: "Pastor Paul. He's the most amazing man. Very accomplished writer. And highly educated. He used to be a Pharisee, you know. We are very lucky to have him. Did you know he is a descendant of the tribe of Benjamin? Not to mention he knows the law better than anyone I've ever seen."

In his letter, it is actually Paul who recounts the accolades about himself, but for a wholly different purpose. It's as if he is intentionally laying out all of his award ribbons before his friends. But then he finishes with these words, in Philippians 3:8 (NIV): "I consider everything a loss compared to the surpassing greatness of knowing Christ Jesus my Lord, for whose sake I have lost all things. I consider them rubbish, that I may gain Christ . . ." A different translation reads, "Yes, everything else is worthless when compared with the infinite value of knowing Christ Jesus my Lord."

I find myself struggling with how to help my kids live for God's glory when they see hundreds of advertisements each day telling them to live for their own gratification. I am fearful of the long-term results in our present school system, both public and private, that puts pressure on teens to be "well-rounded" and to begin thinking about their college résumé starting in middle school. I even feel an uneasiness when our churches encourage teens to "discover who they really are" by identifying their gifts, abilities, and passions without equipping them with gratitude, humility, and a servant's heart that is willing to use those gifts for the benefit of others rather than themselves. I wonder if we are not equipping our kids to be Pauls minus the selflessness.

Writer Mitch Albom said, "The way you get meaning into your life is to devote yourself to loving others, devote yourself to your community around you, and devote yourself to creating something that gives you purpose."[11] His words sound much like what Jesus said when asked what is the most important commandment: To love God with all that you are and to love others as yourself (see Luke 10:27). The only difference is that we don't have to create something to give us purpose. We have each been invited to freely share in his glory.

The Final Scene

I don't pretend to know how to tell you to shepherd your teen into living a passionate life for the glory of God's name—mostly because doing it myself is something I struggle with every day. I'm coming to realize that a life of passion is not something I can instruct my kids in, but rather something I model for them by inviting them into my own journey. It's not so much a "here's how" as it is a "come and discover." After all, I'm not writing their story for them. I'm simply introducing them to the Author and watching the pages unfold.

Our kids are still in the opening chapters of their stories—full of faith, excitement, and risk. Unlike art house films that leave you hanging, every good story has a resolution. A resolution makes sense and gives meaning to the struggles and trials of the characters. Of the resolution part of the story, Donald Miller concludes, "I know the final scene, but not all the acts in between." When I imagine the resolution of my kids' stories, the best final scene I can envision is to hear their heavenly Father say, "Well done, faithful servant." Then they will fully see how their story was connected to God's story.

9

Hello, I'm a Mac

If I live to be a hundred and never see the seven wonders
that'll be alright. If I never make it to the big leagues,
if I never win a Grammy, I'm gonna be just fine.
'Cause I know who I am.

Jessica Andrews[1]

Before he even speaks, you know the words that will flow from
his mouth: "Hello, I'm a Mac." It's one of many TV commercials created by Apple Inc. that are designed to distinguish the
quality of the Mac over the run-of-the-mill PC. Both the stuffy,
overweight office worker and the young, laid-back programmer
are meant to represent computers, but who they are and what
they can do couldn't be more different.

I use a Mac. I was a PC guy my whole life but recently made
the switch. There was a brief learning curve while finding my

way around the new system. But after a couple of weeks I was rolling with no help. A few months later my wife asked me for some help on our home computer—the one represented by the out-of-touch office drone. (I was warned that I, too, would become a Mac snob.) I had forgotten how to do some things. I remember the frustration of trying to get our PC to do what my Mac could do. Or, admittedly, vice versa.

They aren't even remotely alike. I can type a letter, listen to music, and surf the Web on both systems, but how each of them accomplishes those functions is like night and day. They behave, think, look, and respond differently. And when I try to run them both at the same time, it creates nothing but frustration for me.

You probably feel this same kind of tension in your home between you and your teen. And if you have more than one teen, it's like throwing a Palm Pilot in with the two computers. As you think about the blank stares, grunting, rolling eyes, or deafening silence you get when trying to talk to your kid, how many times have you found yourself thinking . . .

—"Why do you have to be so hard-headed?!"
—"If you would just listen to me, you wouldn't get yourself in these messes."
—"There is no way we have the same genes."
—"Why can't you just do what I say?"
—"This is like talking to a brick wall!"

Maybe you've tried talking about some pop-culture issues with your teen, and it turned into a big fight. You wanted to talk about being safe when out with his or her friends, and all you got was a blank stare. Or maybe you wanted to address school study habits and received huffing and grunting in return. At that point, it's easy to say to yourself, "I quit." Or worse, to say to your teen, "Get out of my face."

Don't let the huffing, grunting, and rolling eyes dissuade you from addressing concerns with your teens. Regardless of their response at the moment, they want you to help them and guide them. Their need for security cries out for it. In most cases, it is not your concern that causes the tension. It's the way the issue is addressed.

Just like You?

The way you and your teen respond to the same information can be completely different. It's not necessarily because your kid is obstinate or unteachable. Giving the benefit of the doubt that he or she wants to learn the best way to live, there are some other factors at play that may cause the frustrating responses.

Think about the two computers again. They are both designed to accomplish the same end. Once you put in the information, you have to let them each work through their own process—even though in the end they will both arrive at the same answer.

Similarly, it's not that your kids don't want to learn. More than likely you are trying to put information into them in a way they cannot process. They can listen to you, but they simply cannot hear you. They approach their world according to their unique design—a design that is made up of many elements.

My son and I could not be more different in how we approach life. I like to be in loud places with large groups of people. Bailey would prefer reading a book or playing a board game with a couple of friends. I like adrenaline. Bailey likes security. If we sit down together to play a game, I look for ways to "modify" the rules. He says, "Dad, why can't we just play the way it's supposed to be?"

I walk into every situation with a personal way of perceiving life that God has created for me, a design or "shape" that makes sense to me. If I try to make my son "fit" into my way of solving problems, facing challenges, or living in community with others, I could crush his spirit. I would force him into a personal bondage where there is no freedom to think or explore for himself. He would not be able to be who God has created him to be.

There is a revealing scene in the eighties film classic *The Breakfast Club* where each of the five characters takes turns telling why he or she has been sent to the all-day Saturday detention. The jock, Andrew, confesses that his punishment resulted from publicly humiliating a weaker student. If you haven't seen the movie, I'm not going to share the demoralizing details with you. Needless to say, he is very aware of the shame he has caused another boy. At a certain point, Andrew peels back a layer of emotional protection to let us see inside his heart. He says, "You wanna know why I did it? It's because of my old man." Andrew felt such pressure from his father to be the best athlete, just like his dad. To be a winner even at someone else's expense. He screams as he recalls his father's words, "Win! Win! Win! I won't tolerate any losers in this family!"[2] Andrew looked buff and macho, but on the inside he was a broken boy who felt trapped into being someone he didn't enjoy.

I remember seeing the scene while in high school and thinking, "God, please don't let me grow up to be that kind of dad." Now that I am a dad, I'm even more aware of the dangers that scene exposes. I live with the reality that I am my son's hero. Oddly enough, I feel no arrogance in those words. If anything, it fills me with humility and wonder. I'm amazed that God would give me the privilege, as flawed as I am, of trying to model for him how to be a man. A man who makes time for his family, who watches out for those who are weaker and protects them, who gives value to people by treating them with respect, and who talks highly of his wife.

Being my son's hero also gives me great pause and caution in how I lead him. One night at dinner, he and his sister were talking about what they want to be when they grow up. They listed everything from zookeeper to race car driver to ballerina to cartoonist. I'll let you figure out who said what. Later that night, Bailey came up to me in private and said, "Dad, when I grow up I really want to be a speaker, so I can help people just like you do." This is my son who doesn't like crowds, loud places, or unpredictable environments. I can imagine the damage that could be wrought on him if I pressured him to be just like me. That doesn't mean that he can't follow in my footsteps as a career. But I have to give him freedom, space, and opportunities to discover the world according to how God has made him.

Discovering the Way

In order for your teen to live in his or her culture according to how God has made him or her, it's imperative that you understand them. One of the greatest things you could do is to become a student of your kids. Do you ever find yourself amazed at their uniqueness? At the special ways they contribute to your family? How they respond differently to their world than you do? When I am old and reflect back on my life, I hope I am able to say, "I understood my children."

Proverbs 22:6 (NIV) has been a much-abused and misunderstood verse in regard to child rearing.

> Train a child in the way he should go,
> and when he is old he will not turn from it.

Over the years, I have heard countless sermons on family life in which the teacher has said some variation of "If you teach your children God's word, then when they grow up they will obey it." Many questions come to my mind at hearing this. How do I know if I'm really teaching them God's word or just what I think it is? How much of it do I have to train them in—all of it or just the cool stories? In terms of repetition, how many times do I have to teach it until it sticks? More pointedly, what do I do with all those times in my own life that I've known the truth and simply chosen not to obey? And I don't mean isolated incidents. I'm talking extended periods of disobedience. There has to be more to the verse than may appear. I think there is a better way of understanding this verse, an understanding that both gives freedom of expression and acknowledges God's authority over the process of growth.

The phrase "in the way" is literally translated "according to his way" or "according to his bent."[3] It is not me approaching my kids' lives in the way that makes sense to me. It is me helping make sense of God's truth according to the way God has uniquely designed each of them, and then helping them to embrace that design.

I can't help but think of some of the teen girls my wife has worked with in our church group. These girls are growing up in a culture where they are valued more for the look of their bodies than the content of their brains. They are bombarded with media influences in their lives that tells them they don't look good enough. They need to be taller, skinnier, sexier, whatever. More than 90 percent of the girls in the group are from divorced homes, where Dad is only partly in the picture or gone altogether. For them, each day is defined by survival, not by fulfillment. Teaching truth in this environment is incredibly difficult, because these girls have no idea who God has made them to be. Even when the women in the group would speak words of encouragement and affirmation, they were met with skepticism.

I mentioned earlier that I want to be able to say that I understand my children, but I also want my children to understand themselves. I want them to be comfortable in their own skins, to find joy in the way they are made and how they approach life. This is the freedom of Proverbs 22:6. As I love and teach "according to their way" (God's design), when they grow up they won't walk away from God's design for themselves. They will find freedom in being themselves and see how God's fingerprint on their lives helps them understand how they fit into God's plan.

This means there are going to be differences when it comes to living out truth in their lives. I teach my children the same truth, but it will be understood and applied differently by each of my children because God has made them uniquely different. There is not a one-size-fits-all when it comes to living out truth. Don't misread what I'm saying; truth does not change. It is how it is lived out in a practical way that may be different between my children.

Let's say you are going to help your teenagers understand how to express their faith in everyday life. You bring up James 1:27 in a conversation and present its truth in a way that makes sense to each of them. Your goal is to instruct them in such a way that they feel compelled to go and live out their faith "according to their bent."

You have a son that God has given a natural inclination toward being a protector and showing concern for others. Because he is full of mercy, when he grows to adulthood he decides to adopt a child. In his mind and heart this is the most honest way for him to fulfill this passage. But your daughter is a natural leader. She is a mobilizer with charisma. As she grows up, she starts a nonprofit organization that gathers community leaders together to help provide job opportunities and training to society's forgotten people. Neither expression is better or any more true than the other. If you asked each of them why they were doing what they are doing, they could both say, "Because it is the right thing to do." Both are honoring the injunction to "care for orphans and widows in their distress."

Showing the Way

There are many dynamics of your teenager's life to be understood in order to lead them in their world. Most of these have already been covered in other books by authors who said it better than I could, and their books are well worth reading. Instead of trying to add to their work, I thought it better to recommend them and let you read them in their own words.

The Five Love Languages of Teenagers by Gary Chapman has provided a wealth of knowledge on understanding how teenagers feel and express love. If you are going to start with one book, this should be it. Ross Campbell's book *How to Really Love Your Teen* is similar in content but also deals with teen anger and its causes.

Cynthia Tobias has written several books that help you understand both childhood and adolescent learning processes. Her book *The Way They Learn* is priceless in explaining different learning styles and helping you help your teen learn more effectively.

Gary Smalley is the king of personalities and relationships. His book with John Trent, *The Two Sides of Love*, doesn't specifically address parent–teen relationships, but the truths easily apply here. It will help you understand personality differences and see the strengths in your teen's personality. If you have younger children, *The Treasure Tree* brings personalities down to a child's level.

Kanakuk Kamps director Joe White has been writing about teenagers for as long as I can remember. His book *Wired by God* is the best I've ever read on helping your teenager set goals, discover their abilities, and make a plan for the future.

I can't express enough how important these issues are in understanding your teenager. If you can't identify your teenager's personality, communicate love in a way your teen can receive it, or understand the learning style of your teen, you'll need to do some research on these subjects. I want to add to them by looking at the parts of your teen's life we have already talked about and see how they can affect how you lead.

All the Right Pieces

I've always felt closer to God's heart when outdoors. Those early years as a camp director broadened my understanding of how to captivate teenagers with God's bigness through nature. Since then my wife and I have taken countless teen groups on outdoor trips. By far, my favorite is spelunking. There is something about taking teenagers to a place they've never been before. Showing them wonders they wouldn't get to experience unless they were underground walking step by step with me through the darkness.

"How do I put this thing on?" can be heard many times by teens as they reach for the harnesses we've dropped at their feet. With much patience, Mona shows each of them how to get their legs through the woven pretzel. Even though they have worn many hats by this age, they usually need help putting on the helmets as well. I always laugh when a kid asks what the "clippy thing" (a carabiner) is for. At this point, they have all the equipment they need, but if we didn't show them how to use it, they could never go farther than the mouth of the cave. All of them could probably easily maneuver through the dark in their own houses to find the bathroom at night, but none of them have ever experienced the darkness of a deep cave. This is a new kind of blackness that requires someone to lead them through it, even with flashlights. In the end, the result is always the same. After spending hours moving slowly one step at a time through the narrow tunnels and slippery rocks, they emerge back into the warmth of the sunlight with a smile, saying, "That's the coolest thing I've ever done!"

Going into it, I know the level of trust required from students to let me lower them with ropes over darkened ledges or to follow me through a two-foot tunnel when they don't know where it will lead. As a guide, I've learned one crucial lesson. This more challenging kind of experience always goes smoother toward the end of a trip. Once students have followed us through less risky excursions, they are more willing to trust us with the new, more daunting challenge.

Every day of their lives, teenagers are going through new experiences. In some of the situations, they have no sure bearings. They have no firm foothold. But they do have all the equipment they need. Our job is to help them know how to take the equipment of their life and make sense of it, so that they can walk into the situation with a certain excitement and expectation of success.

One piece of equipment is the values instilled in them by God. They don't want to be anyplace where their values aren't affirmed. Take some time and think through how you can affirm each of the values you see in their lives, and give them opportunities to live them out in healthy ways.

For example, you can affirm their need for community by enabling them to be in situations where healthy relationships can occur. When your daughter wants to set up a MySpace page to talk with friends, you can affirm her need for community but still teach her healthy boundaries for online behavior. When your son wants to go out driving with friends on Friday night, you can affirm his need for time with them but still set expectations of what is right behavior when with his friends.

By creating an environment in your home where you celebrate diversity, you affirm that you value authenticity. When they are going through difficulties with friends or feel embarrassed with a failure, you get to help them share their feelings. In doing so, you show them that you value realness and transparency. When you invite them into your spiritual journey by praying together, you are telling them that you are in process too. Sharing what God is teaching you and inviting them to do the same can be one of the most intimate and authentic moments you can have with your teenager.

As you lead your teens to live in God's world, you get to help them discover their passions. What are the interests that seem to breathe life into them? Regardless of the careers they choose, the causes they rally around, or the particular concern that resonates with them, it can all be done to bring God glory.

The more you understand their personalities, see how they express love to others, and provide opportunities for their values to thrive, the more you will understand how to open up their passions. For instance, my son is quite the bookworm, so I invited him to come with me to teach younger children as part of a tutoring program. Both our kids enjoy serving others, so my wife took them to help decorate a classroom for a friend who is a schoolteacher. We are trying to find things that resonate with them to see whether a passion emerges. If it's not there, it's okay. We'll keep providing more opportunities to explore and to be who God has made them until they have their *Braveheart* moment and feel compelled to do something. And when that day happens, we'll both be there to cheer them along for his glory.

Hopefully, you've spent some time thinking about the kind of influence you can have in your teens' lives. You are the greatest long-term influence, but the quality of that influence is solely up to you. Either you can be distracted by the petty, temporal influences around them and focus your energies on "going to war" against them, or you can spend your time lovingly walking alongside your teens. You can't effectively divide your attention between two places.

Influence is gained over time—long periods of it. I had to gain influence with campers by spending time with them in other situations before taking them caving. The same is true of you with your teens. The more influence you earn, the more they will trust you in new situations. Your kids will not let you lead them into being who God has made them to be if they do not trust you. Show them that you are trustworthy by responding with grace when they confess their struggles. Show them that they can entrust their hearts to you by responding with compassion during their hurts. Show them that they can trust you with their relationships by treating their friends with respect.

The Pages of Their Lives

It is easy to fall into the trap of thinking, "If I can just put together all the pieces of the puzzle, then I'll have a picture of who my teen really is." This is how we were taught to approach life. Take a test to determine your aptitudes, then answer some questions that pinpoint your strengths, then add to that a computer program on relationships, and "voila." Out come the results that tell you that you should be a mechanical engineer. I think tests and assessments can pinpoint some indicators and help narrow the possibilities, but life is not that cut-and-dried. You run the risk of limiting where God may be leading your teens by assuming a plot on a matrix can tell you more about them than they can with their own words.

Our teens are part of a culture with far more opportunities for self-expression and possibility than we ever had. They are part of a culture of imagination, where dabbling in multiple areas is encouraged. There is something to be said for the kid who at a young age knows what he or she wants from the future and takes steps during adolescence to someday become that person. But understand that this is not today's typical teenager. Most teens today have a broader scope for their futures than we did growing up. I don't think they try many different things because they are afraid to commit to something. Rather, they are looking at our lives as adults and don't want to commit to the wrong things. As we walk with them through their world and help them discover who they really are, the pieces of their puzzles begin to fall into place.

One year our family spent a week in Branson, Missouri, on vacation. After rejecting much of the entertainment fare Branson had to offer, we found one show that we all enjoyed—The Kirby VanBurch Magic Show.[4] VanBurch had all the "suspended reality moments" one would hope to see at a magic show. He changed into a roaring tiger one minute and walked through glass the next. The climax of the show was making a helicopter appear out of thin air. I have no idea how many times during the show I said, "How did he do that?"

In the middle of these complex and amazing feats, Kirby did a rather simple illusion involving a coloring book and a little boy. He gave the book to the boy and explained that it was a "special" coloring book. As he flipped through the pages we could all see the black outline drawings, just like any other coloring book waiting to be colored in. He then flipped through the pages a second time as the little boy waved his hands over the book. This time all the pictures were colored in. Then, in typical magician style, VanBurch took it one step further, telling the boy that the great thing about the coloring book was he could always start over. This time as he flipped through the pages, they were all blank. And of course I said, "How did he do that?"

I found out after the show that the trick depends on where you flip open the coloring book. Some pages are black-and-white, some are colored, and others are blank. It made me think about our teenagers. All of the various kinds of pages are in their lives as well. We just need to give them space to explore and freedom to be who God made them. As we do, the different pages will appear, some with vibrant colors and others with muted tones. Some of the colors will even appear outside of the lines, and that's okay. God gives us the privilege of helping shape some of the pictures, but *he has already made the design*. Wouldn't it be amazing if years from now when your teenagers are grown and reflecting back on their lives, they said, "My mom (or dad) helped the pictures of who I am jump right off the pages"?

PART 3

ENGAGING THE
WORLD TOGETHER

10

Melted Gummi Bears
(and other thoughts on loving people)

The problem with Christian culture is we think of love as a commodity. We use it like money. I could see it clearly, and I could feel it in the pages of my life. This was the thing that had smelled so rotten all those years. I used love like money. The church used love like money.

Donald Miller[1]

Grocery shopping is a family event in our house. My wife takes one basket while the rest of us take another. Over the years I've learned that if I want to make it home with certain items, it works better to have my own basket. Mona picks out all the fruits and vegetables while the rest of the gang searches out the good stuff like hot dogs, Pop-Tarts, and potato chips. Every once in a while we'll splurge and head over to the candy aisle.

The usual item—gummi bears. A five-pound bag. It may sound like a lot, but a sugar-happy dad with two kids can throw down some gummi bears!

I was getting ready for a road trip in a couple of days and decided this would be the sugar of choice to keep me awake while driving. The only problem was that we left the candy in the van overnight. After two days of sweltering Memphis heat, all that was left in the bag was one giant blob of gelatin in a kaleidoscope of colors. It looked like a Brach's candy troll had thrown up in the bag.

You'd better believe I didn't let this opportunity go to waste. I mean, how many times in your life can you say you ate a five-pound gummi bear? I started trying to pull the outside bears away from blob. They would come off, but parts of a few other bears would come as well. If I pulled a red bear, it would come away with a yellow foot and green hand. And so on. No matter how many I pulled apart, it was always the same result.

This is what happens when we are in real community with others. We become so much a part of the lives of those around us that a melding of lives happens. Their story becomes our story. Their pain and joy becomes our pain and joy. Their experiences become part of our own. This kind of community takes a significant investment of time and selflessness. At times, it requires me to die to my own agenda in order to be with those around me.

Jesus didn't tell us to wave politely to our neighbors as we pull into the driveway. He tells us to get out of the car, forget about the groceries and mail for a moment, walk across the yard, and spend some time loving them. He tells us to invite them into our homes for dinner, take vacations together, and serve them in their times of need. He didn't use so many words. Jesus simply said, "Love each other. Just as I have loved you, you should love each other" (John 13:34).

Some teachers might argue that Jesus was talking only to the disciples when he said this. Perhaps he was, but the example of his life was evidence of the kind of love he was talking about. He was talking about a kind of love that is willing to meet an adulterous woman in public. The kind of love that follows a repentant tax collector to his home for a party, or sits with a blind and broken man beside a pool and listens to his story. Wherever there were people that were in need, Jesus knew his love would be welcome.

As people who follow this Jesus, we are called to love in the same way. In fact, this is the kind of faith that our teens are looking for in us. They want us to lead them into the culture in such a way that they can be salt and light. They want us to show them an active faith full of risky adventures, loving others made in God's image. To do this we have to be willing to engage the world together as a family.

It's easy for me to allow the youth pastor at our church to take my son or daughter on a mission trip, so that he will learn to serve others. It's easy for me to go on a service project to the Gulf Coast with a bunch of men. But it's much harder for me to do this as a family. At times it's hard for me to figure out how I take my culture and my kids' culture and move together into our world.

I wonder if it's because there were never meant to be all these different cultures. Maybe we were never meant to label and classify one another the way we do. All of our labeling seems to leave us with only two options—one right and one wrong. Conservative or liberal. Contemporary or traditional. Christian or secular. Grown-up or teenaged.

There is a lot of talk in churches now about worldviews. For the most part it has been a healthy exercise for discussing the nature of truth and how to live it out. Unfortunately, most of those in the church boil it all down to two worldviews—a

Christian and a secular. The difference is simple and basic. There is a good one and an evil one. But does that mean that the person who doesn't embrace the entire prescription must be wrong, living a lie, or evil? What if the parts they disagree on aren't theological issues, but social ones? What if they follow the same Christ, but their expression of faith looks very different from your own?

There has to be a different way of seeing the value in people than by their agreement with the prescripts of orthodox Christian faith. For those of us in the church, the question is not, "Do they believe the truth?" Rather the question should be, "Does my heart love regardless of what they believe?" *If we do not first love, then we cannot expect to be heard.* Donald Miller said, "If a person senses that you do not like them, that you do not approve of their existence, then your religion and your political ideas will all seem wrong to them."[2] The same is true if those in our culture think we are only with them to try to change them, to bring them over to our side and convince them we are right.

This doesn't diminish the truth or our mandate from Christ to live out and teach truth. Instead it places truth (and morality) squarely in the context of relationships. We begin to see life as relationships and community with others. We see—better yet our culture sees—the truth as love being lived out among them. As we become like melted gummi bears—loving as we have been loved—there is a transfer of values. As our hearts are melded into the lives of those around us, there is a willingness to show mercy and understanding.

I know the kind of people Jesus enjoyed being in community with because I see them in my own life. People like the men in white shirts and black ties that ride their bikes around my neighborhood. People like the neighborhood kids who knock on our door, what seems like every fifteen minutes. People like the unkempt man standing at the intersection asking for help.

Some time ago, we were taking our kids to my parents' house for the weekend when we pulled up to a red light. My son, then eight, said, "Dad, why is that man standing there?" The man he pointed to was wearing worn army fatigues and holding a sign that read, "Please help." No matter how many times I diverted my eyes, he was still there.

All of a sudden the struggle begins. There is a pull to stay on course with my agenda for the day, and another pull to be detoured by love for another. And not just a love for the homeless man, but a love for my son. A kind of love that demonstrates how to love others. A kind of love that shows him it is worth the few dollars and the few minutes it will take to go through the drive-through and get a meal for another person. Because I love my son, I show him how to love the stranger.

The People in My Neighborhood

Our backyard covers about twelve acres. I guess it would be more accurate to say that our back lawn butts up against a county park, so we like to think of the park as part of one big backyard. There's not really much more there than a worn-out tennis court, some rusted playground equipment, and a boarded-up bathhouse. But for us, our "backyard" is like a modern-day marketplace for the neighborhood, where everyone meets and gets to know one another.

When we moved in several years ago, we decided against putting up a privacy fence. We're still the only ones who haven't. But it was about more than having easy access to a swing set. We also didn't want to block people from us. We love being able to sit in our backyard and see everything that's happening in the park. Most of the people in our neighborhood became friends by spending time in that park.

I know we won't always live here, but while we do we've taught our kids that our family has a responsibility to our little park. One weekend we had a group of teenagers from a local church come over and repaint the equipment, pick up trash, and plant some trees. Once a month our family walks around the park picking up trash. We've even gotten other families involved in helping to build benches, repair a basketball court, and erect soccer goals.

Last year word began to spread that the county was going to sell the park to a developer for a nice profit. The whole neighborhood was buzzing. We had neighborhood meetings, mostly to vent frustration but also to mobilize ourselves. People began to write letters to the mayor. The sheriff came to meet with our neighborhood group. Several of us called the news stations and newspapers. Our kids even got their picture in the paper playing in the park. Within a couple of weeks, the mayor was interviewed by the local paper and let everyone know they were no longer planning to sell the park. I'm sure to most of the people in our city, it wasn't that big of a deal. But for the fifty or so families in our neighborhood, it made us feel like a community. We had something in common to believe in.

The spiritual beliefs of our neighbors have never been an issue with our family. Instead, we've tried hard to teach our kids that they have a responsibility to love people regardless of where they're coming from. Period. How they live and what the people are like is not a stipulation for loving them. We love them because they are members of our community.

A few years ago our family hosted a neighborhood cookout. Another neighbor and I pulled our grills out into the park, and everyone brought their favorite meats. There were kids running around everywhere playing games while moms and dads kicked back in lawn chairs. We had everyone from newborns to grandparents joining us. It looked like a snapshot from a small Baptist church outdoor potluck.

However, there was one major difference. One of our neighbors at the time was a middle-aged guy with a Harley. Every time I saw him, he looked like he walked out of a motorcycle showroom, with his black leather jacket, dark glasses, torn jeans, and thick mustache-goatee combo. Our Harley neighbor came riding into the park on his motorcycle with a big keg on the back. I don't think it went unnoticed by anyone. So there we were with hamburgers, key lime pies, a mess of kids, and a keg on the back of a Harley.

For him, it was just his way of being a part of the festivities. In his mind it was an appropriate gift to say, "Thanks for including me." So we received him and his keg just as we did the missionary couple that brought their favorite (nonalcoholic) dessert.

Instead of us always being the ones reaching out to them, there have been times my neighbors have taught me how a Christian should love. Our next-door neighbors, Ernesto and Yuridia, are from Mexico. When they first moved in, Yuridia could speak only a few words of English, and we communicated mostly through smiles and waves. Ernesto, on the other hand, is quite fluent, and at every opportunity we've tried to learn from one another.

During some recent debates on immigration reform, I'd watch countless politicians get camera time to share their passionate positions on the evils of illegal immigration. Then I'd think about my neighbor and all he has gone through to give his family a better life. He gets up every morning and works harder than I do to make sure his daughters have a nice home and good education. He runs his own company and helps other young Mexican men get financially established in a new country. When you live in community with people like Ernesto, the political lines become less rigid, because you start seeing the people themselves and not just a political position.

When Ernesto's little girl turned four, they invited our family over for a birthday party. One thing I've learned about the Latino culture is that no celebration is small. I loved being invited and letting my kids see how others celebrate life. But I experienced an odd feeling while I was there.

Out of the twenty-plus people that were there, Ernesto and my family were the only ones who spoke English. I got to practice the ten Spanish phrases I know, but mostly I did a lot of smiling and nodding that day. No one introduced themselves to us, not because they were rude, but because they simply didn't know how. The language barrier was uncomfortable for all of us. I couldn't begin to guess what food we ate that day—some kind of spicy meat in a tortilla. What I remember most about the meal was my children sitting in my lap feeling uneasy about being strangers among all these people that seemed to know one another.

As we were walking home, I was struck that what I was feeling must be how someone outside the church feels whenever they interact with Christians. The beat of the music sounds familiar, but the words make no sense. They can't decipher the lingo we've created. Everyone seems to move in herds past them, busily going about their spiritual activities. When their eyes meet ours, there is an unfamiliarity—a discomfort—so we just smile and wave. Rarely do we take the time to engage them in meaningful conversation, to listen in such a way that says, "The most important thing to me right now is hearing your story." When you begin to move into community with those people, you become very aware of the unintentional obstacles in your life that keep people from opening up.

A few months ago a new family moved in across the street—a single African American mom with twins. Her girls are around the same age as our daughter, so there was an immediate connection over Polly Pockets. Within a couple of weeks, the girls were all playing together at our house or in the park. Just as

Mona and I were trying to get to know the mom, we walked out of our house one morning to see racial slurs scrawled on her fence. I felt an overwhelming helplessness as I stood at her door with homemade cookies, trying to speak words of encouragement. When you live in community with someone who is still being judged because of skin color, you realize racial and social issues are more vital than you may once have thought.

I've told our kids more times than I can remember that heaven looks like our neighborhood. We've had single moms with live-in boyfriends, families from Venezuela, Mexico, and the Philippines, Harley riders, missionaries, drug dealers, retired couples, African Americans, and Asians. And then there is our family, as best we know how trying to be like melted gummi bears, experiencing life with these people. I wish I could say that our family knows what we are doing and have a plan in all this, but we don't. Every day we have to make choices about engaging people, just as you do. We are trying to adopt a lifestyle that allows us to show them what God's world is like and how we can be part of it. Showing openness to our neighbors is one way that my wife and I try to open our children's hearts and minds to the world outside them. There are other ways. We have taken our kids to Mexico to let them see what life is like in a different culture. We've served meals together at a homeless shelter and talked about how to show respect to all people. I've taken my son with me to help tutor and read to Sudanese refugee children, and talked with him about life on the other side of the world. These all seem like small things to me, but they represent the best way I know how to stretch the hearts and imaginations of our teenagers.

Jesus said that all the requirements of the Hebrew law are fulfilled when we love God and our neighbors (Matthew 22:40). By "neighbors," he didn't just mean the people we see at church on Sunday mornings. He means everyone—from the Islamic boy on my son's basketball team to the man down the street whose political yard sign shows preferences I don't endorse. We don't love these neighbors out of obligation or as a project. We love because our Creator chose to reach his hand into his creation and redeem our family. Now we have the privilege of taking that redeeming love to those around us.

Whether your family is in the heart of the city, a suburban gated development, or a rural farm, it is possible for you to love those around you. It doesn't have to look like my family's experience. It will simply be you helping your teenagers to live out their values and passions as an influence in their world. And you don't have to travel halfway around the world to do this. Start right where you are. On the next two pages are a few ideas of ways to engage the culture together, as a family.

These are just a few things my family or others I know have tried. This doesn't mean that you should go and try all of them. They are just meant to spur your thinking.

This is going to take some real work on your part (and that of your whole family) to think and pray through how God would have you respond to the culture you live in. Take some time at dinner to think through this together. Use the few minutes in the car with your middle schooler to talk about these issues.

I should also note that doing any of the ideas listed (or any you may come up with) can be *extremely* threatening for teenagers. Not because teenagers don't like to love, but because they aren't used to doing it *with you*. They will not be willing to go along with you on any of this if you have not earned their trust. Also, this is not the time to parent them. This is *their* expression of love. Let them show it or say it however they need to. It may look or feel different from how you would do it.

What your family does together doesn't have to be big or make it onto your local news. All God is looking for is sincerity, humility, and selflessness. Not fireworks. Take the resources

Engaging Your Community

- Watch a film or documentary concerning a current social issue, then talk about ways to respond.[3]
- Work on a building project together.[4]
- Volunteer to serve in a community service organization.[5]
- Invite a couple of families that don't attend church to join with you in providing a Thanksgiving meal for a needy family.
- Invite someone of a different culture to your home to show you how they celebrate different events (e.g., Christmas, Thanksgiving, New Year's Eve).

Engaging Your Neighborhood

- Take a walk around the block, stopping to introduce yourselves to neighbors you've never met.
- Host a cookout for three families on the block.
- Take a "Welcome to the Neighborhood" package to a new family.
- When a neighbor has a new baby, take the whole family over to cut the grass, make a meal, and run errands.
- Hang a white sheet in the backyard, and host a neighborhood movie night for the kids.
- Write a letter to a neighborhood family expressing appreciation for their friendship.

Questions to Provoke Love

How has God created you to be able to love those you meet every day?

What do you do that breathes life into you—that really gets you going?

If you could go serve people anywhere in the world, where would you go and what would you do?

What do you like about our neighborhood, community, city, etc.?

How can teenagers make a difference in the lives of those around them?

When you think about your school, what kind of a difference would it make if it were a place where people valued and respected one another? What part can you play in that?

Jesus tells us to love "the least of these." Who would you say those people are in our community, and what part can our family play in loving them?

Isaiah 1:17 says to "seek justice, encourage the oppressed" (NIV). What issues of justice in our community can your family be a part of?

What small thing could you do today to make someone feel loved?

If you moved tomorrow, what would you hope those in our neighborhood would say about you when you're gone?

If you could spend two hours a week making a difference in someone else's life, what would you want to do?

you have, the abilities of your teens, and the passions God has placed in their hearts, and go love.

Chances are your teens won't have to be convinced to love others. They are just looking for you to take the initiative to lead them into something that will capture their hearts and imaginations.

Go and let your heart connect with those around you. Let your teenagers experience God's love flowing out of your family. Let them see that it is possible to love God and their world.

Be like melted gummi bears.

11

Boating Upstream

I have one life and one chance to make it count for something. . . . I'm free to choose what that something is, and the
something I've chosen is my faith. Now, my faith goes beyond theology and religion and requires considerable work
and effort. My faith demands—this is not optional—my faith
demands that I do whatever I can, wherever I am, whenever
I can, for as long as I can with whatever I have to try to make
a difference.

President Jimmy Carter[1]

My entire life has been lived near the Mississippi River. When
you stand on its wide banks watching the waters rush by, there
are two thoughts that run through your mind: this river is

powerful, and this river is dirty. It is a fast-moving cauldron of silt and murky brown water deserving of its name, the Big Muddy.

It's not just the thick silt turning over as the waters surge past its banks that makes the river dirty. Primarily it's the trash. Along some stretches you are likely to see more plastic soda bottles, wooden crates, and old newspapers than fish.

A few years ago I read a story about Chad Pregracke, who was so upset with the trash in the river he made it his personal mission to clean it up.[2] He got tired of seeing the place he loves littered with everything imaginable. So at twenty-one he set out in a small boat to cruise the upper Mississippi picking up trash. The first season he personally picked up 45,000 pounds of trash. The next year he founded Living Lands & Waters,[3] recruited a cleanup crew, and secured corporate sponsorship.

Each spring, after the last bit of river ice has melted, this ragtag group of folks load up on a used tugboat and two barges that were salvaged from the bottom of the Ohio River. In the first five years, the group has hauled in more than one million pounds of trash. So far they've collected over 14,000 tires, 1,200 steel drums, 600 plastic drums, 500 refrigerators, 350 propane tanks, 49 kitchen sinks, and enough Styrofoam to cover a football field two feet deep. One day Pregracke even found a cooler with a horse's head inside. But still, day after day, they pull trash by hand from the riverbank muck.

I saw a similar news story on ABC about these families that live on a dirty bayou. The families were so frustrated with the stuff floating around in their waters that they all built fences in the water to try and keep the trash away from their homes. Made of orange webbing, the barriers looked like mini-construction sites in the water. Speaking of the mess, one home owner said, "We've tried to get it out, but there is just too much. At this point in time, we're just trying to keep it away."

The two responses couldn't be more different. On one hand, you have people who live on the river who don't like the trash but are willing to ignore it as long as their little piece of paradise is safe. Then you have Chad, who starts at the bottom of a river, working his way upstream. And he's not just cleaning—he's educating people as his tug moves upward. As Chad has shared his mission in countless school presentations, town meetings, and news stories, others are picking up the cause. Now there are restoration projects on the Illinois, Ohio, Potomac, and Anacostia rivers.

I see a disturbing similarity with many Christians today. All around I see Christians who have built protective barriers around their homes and hearts. As long as they are safe, who cares if the culture rots? Instead of engaging the world around them, they have created their own subculture with their own bookstores, conferences, music, T-shirts, and lingo and wrapped it all in an orange webbing barrier to keep it clean and protected. In *The Externally Focused Church*, authors Rick Rusaw and Eric Swanson say,

> Traditionally, when Christians haven't liked what's going on in schools, they've started their own schools. If they didn't like what was happening in some business organizations, they began their own. When they didn't like secular music, they created their own industry. As a result, we now have "Christian" versions of nearly everything. Instead of influencing the cultural stream, we've created our own parallel stream.[4]

In other words, we aren't trying to clean up the cultural river anymore. Instead, we've dug our own channel right next to it. The funny thing is how remarkably similar are the values of the two rivers, except we've labeled one "Christian." It was a reactionary choice of the last generation of Western Christians that has left our culture anemic of truth and desperate for love. We must now make a choice to either run from or redeem. Engagement and escape are our only two options. Building a parallel river is not a response of love. Theologian John Stott put it this way:

> Escape means turning our backs on the world in rejection, washing our hands of it and steeling our hearts against its agonized cries for help. In contrast, engagement is turning our faces toward the world in compassion, getting our hands dirty, sore and worn in its service, and feeling deep within us the stirring of the love of God which cannot be contained.[5]

All of our talk of family values will fall on deaf ears unless others in our culture see us serving and loving as families. We must wade into the murky waters of our culture with our teens, boating upstream, looking for lives to love and redeem. Mark Driscoll said,

> Classic fundamentalists look at the stream and say, "It's all dirty and polluted. Who cares?" But millions of people drink from the stream . . . We have to move as far upstream as we can so the culture is influenced by kingdom people and kingdom values and that the millions of people downstream who are participating in culture are not just drinking polluted water, that they have some fresh streams to choose from.[6]

We know what the fresh water is, or, as Christ calls himself, the "living water." The question is whether or not we will have the heart to engage our culture so that it, too, can see him.

A Story of Hope

I have a friend, Eli Morris, who works at a suburban church in Memphis. God has been using him for many years to create an environment for families to engage their community. He is taking the hearts of his people upstream to clean not just their culture but their own hearts as well. His willingness to model for his own teenagers a different way of loving others has helped make it practical and concrete for me in my family.[7]

Eli has always been a bit of an enigma since God got hold of his heart. He spent several years on staff with Young Life, a campus outreach ministry, as the Memphis Director of Urban Ministries. During this time Young Life clubs were popping up on every other suburban and private high school campus. And then there was Eli, the long-haired sixties-throwback, venturing into new territory in the inner city. He recruited a group of wide-eyed college students to go with him into the forgotten schools to love students otherwise not given much attention or chance of making it. Over the years his team went to hundreds of football games, school lunches, and Bible studies. And who knows how many students were given a chance to go to a Young Life Camp because of all the hard work of that team.

God was using those years with Young Life to root Eli's heart deeply in the culture and lives of the inner-city community. All the while, God was readying Eli for what he was about to unfold.

On the other side of town, about as far away as one could get from the inner city, a new church was being planted, called Hope Presbyterian Church, or just Hope Church to those that know her. Even though the church was planted in a high-growth, economically prosperous part of town, its members wanted to do things a bit differently. They wanted to look outward.

Shortly after the plant, Eli was asked to come on board as the pastor of Urban Ministries.

North Memphis, dotted with its mom-and-pop stores, overgrown yards, and substandard housing, has long been one of the most economically depressed areas of the city. Chain stores left this part of town to follow the economic growth out east, leaving behind schoolyards more littered with trash than smiling children. To Eli, it looked like a place where the heart of God was beating, so he readied the people of Hope Church to accept God's mandate to love and serve the poor in North Memphis.

Eli said, "When you are geographically removed from the poor, you become emotionally removed from them as well." It just doesn't work to sit in a suburban church and talk about the poor and expect the hearts of people to be changed. Eli felt that the only way those who have so much could understand the lives of "the least of these" would be to experience life with them.

If we are going to love others, Stott says, it requires a "willingness to renounce the comfort and security of our own cultural background in order to give ourselves in service to people of another culture, whose needs we may never before have known or experienced."[8] This is the outward-focused life that Hope Church was praying for.

To show people that kind of life, Eli started a program called Urban Plunge. It is an opportunity for adults to experience a taste of life in the inner city over a three-day period. Many of those who decide to "take the plunge" come expecting to do some sort of service project. They come with good intentions to try and make a difference, but in the end it is they who become the students. Eli describes the Urban Plunge as "go and learn, not go and do." They learn to be, before they learn to do.

Over the weekend the thirty or so adults stay at an inner-city ministry on roll-away cots, tour the National Civil Rights Museum, and visit several ministries working in the community. During the Saturday night panel discussion on racism, many come face-to-face with their presuppositions of the poor and those of other cultures. As they sit and listen to the stories of those that have been marginalized by our school systems, government, and churches, something happens. God begins a long-awaited refining. Eli told me, "The hope is that a new world will be opened up to them. They will begin to see people and not issues. They will see past the political perspectives of the left and right when it comes to the poor and begin to see real people." As these suburban visitors to the inner-city look into the eyes of those in front of them, they begin to see people as brothers and sisters. Though their skin may be different, their stories are being woven together into a community of one.

Since 1991 hundreds of people have gone on an Urban Plunge and come home looking at our culture through a different lens. For them it's no longer just a poverty problem. It's a personal problem as well. Part of their heart now lives in North Memphis. Their experiences are giving way to the "new world" Eli has been hoping for.

Maybe you are thinking, "Great story. But what does that have to do with me?" We've spent all this time trying to understand our world and our teens so we can go and lead them in God's world to love others. The reality is, your teens will not let you lead them where you have not been. There is a level of trust that has to be earned. You have been called by God to lead your teens, but they will not follow unless they see the heart they desire inside you. If you don't love, show compassion, or respect those in our culture, your teen is not about to listen as you tell them to go do it.

Many of the adults who have gone on an Urban Plunge have been parents just like you. Eli said the amazing thing has been how many of them come home and say to their kids, "You have got to be part of this with me." They have experienced something that is undeniable in their eyes. Something good has happened to their hearts, and now they want their teens to be a part of it with them. Whole families are now going out to serve the community together.

Hope Church has adopted an inner-city elementary school as part of their own. Entire families show up week after week to read to kids, throw class parties, host appreciation dinners for teachers, and paint classrooms. They've also started basketball camps and sponsored urban movie nights and concerts. Talk about a shared experience with your teenager! These parents are able to take their kids because they've first gone themselves. And now serving has become a part of the culture of their families.

The act of serving together is not the point. It is the change in worldview and priorities that happens in your teen when you go out into the world together. Eli ended our conversation with this thought: "It is not the responsibility of the government, or the school system, or even the church to teach my kids compassion toward the poor. It is my job! How you live with them [the homeless] and how you love them will be the same for your teen." The same principle applies to how your teen will respond to all types of people in their culture.

Engaging people in your culture as a family is the safest, healthiest, and most transferable way for your teenager to learn to love others. Can you see your teenagers living out their values with you as you lead them into loving others? When you walk with them into situations you provide the security they look for. As you introduce them to new people and opportunities, you provide the community and passion they need. As you serve alongside them and love others together, they see the authenticity in your own life and grow in that genuineness themselves.

There is a group of families at Hope Church that know it is possible. They have tasted that kind of life for themselves and are helping introduce this next generation of teens to a more complete way of "being in the world."

12

Employed by Playboy

Sex researchers have long known that teenagers often compromise their moral standards because not to do so would put their popularity at risk.

Tony Campolo[1]

"But how far can we go?" This was the question my wife and I were asking one another during a conversation in the car. It was one of those hypothetical-situation conversations about our kids. We were talking about their future and how much we could encourage them to be part of their culture. Is there anything that's off-limits? Are there situations of which a Christian just can't be a part? When does one stop being an influence? We joked about the possibility of our son became a pro wrestler named the "Holy Avenger" or an Abercrombie & Fitch model (don't think it'll ever happen). But then I said,

"Okay, what if Ashlan were a famous interior decorator and lived out her faith in the design world? Let's say her designs are in all the home magazines, and top celebrities call to have her decorate their homes. Then one day Hugh Hefner calls and says he wants her to come and create a new design for his offices at the Playboy Mansion. Would we encourage her to go?"

After we cringed together about the absurdity of such scenarios, Mona turned to me with complete seriousness and said, "We could, if that is clearly what God was telling her to do." We both nodded, gave each other the reassuring look that says, "We're in this together," and the conversation drifted off.

There wasn't much more to say after that. We drove for a while longer, quietly contemplating the reality that one day our kids will grow up and fully become part of their world. They'll make decisions every day, influenced only in part by us—to engage people, walk in community with others, and live out truth. Regardless of the situation, we'll support their choices if those decisions allow them to live out a fuller expression of who God has made them to be and enable them to be used for his kingdom.

I don't keep the world at bay with a big stick for fear of my kids going off the deep end or walking away from their faith. I know there will be times in their lives when each of them will struggle with honoring God and listening to godly wisdom. They will push the limits of what is healthy and right. And sometimes they will blatantly make wrong choices. They do it now in our home—why would I expect different when they are grown? My goal is not to keep them from ever making mistakes. I hope they do make a few mistakes. It's the only way most of us learn and grow. I don't mean that in a sadistic sense. I don't take joy in seeing my children fail. I simply mean

I hope that even through their missteps they will be able to learn God's design for life.

Don't Even Think about It

Parents play a complex job—on one hand protecting our teens from obvious dangers, and on the other not sheltering them from real-life situations. As they grow older and move into situations we can't control, we trust the Holy Spirit to remind them of truths we have taught and modeled.

If I try to protect them too much, chances are that one of two things will happen. The "thing" that is forbidden becomes alluring, like a magnet drawing them toward it. Or worse, they never learn to exercise their own faith, and soon they grow tired of its standards. When I speak at conferences on teen culture, I sometimes encounter parents who want to tell me all the things their teen has never done. They make glowing statements like:

—"I'm so glad my son has never gone to a school dance."

—"My daughter has never gotten wrapped up in the whole boy thing."

—"We don't even have a computer in our house, so pornography has never really been an issue with our son."

Parents say these kinds of things with much pride. But I've never quite understood this kind of response from parents. That's usually the point where I raise my eyebrows, weakly smile, and say, "Oh, that's great." What's really going through my mind are faces of students I've known whose beliefs were not at all what their parents thought. The faces of two types of students still leave me sad.

163

There were those students who felt shunned or guilt-tripped into "being good." There was no time (or place) for questioning issues of faith. For them, a religious experience was little more than blind obedience. Do what is right. Stop doing what is wrong. Stay away from sinful people and places.

Then there were other students whose "faith" was a clever deception that kept their parents' watchful eyes from looking too closely. These students had the lingo down and followed the rules, but only as a means to an end. Their illusion merely gained the trust and approval of those around them.

For many of these students, college was such a shock to their system that they didn't have much of a chance for a healthy experience. Their exposure to excess, coupled with a lack of support, led to an inability to make real-life choices— and a moral meltdown. They were never taught to think critically about their faith and how it might intersect with God's world. They never learned to see the value in different people's opinions and yet stay true to their own chosen course. Instead they opted for being good because it is what got them love from Mom and Dad, and respect from others. But it worked only as long as they were under their parents' wings.

Don't misunderstand. I think it is best for teenagers to stay away from unhealthy situations. My wife and I actively pray for our children's sexual purity. We pray that their decisions would honor God, others, and themselves. We steer them toward healthy relationships and have shown them the value of integrity and honesty. It will be an answer to prayer if my own kids make it through their adolescent years with their heads and hearts intact. But we don't work toward this by manipulating with guilt or steering them away from every possible learning experience.

We've had many conversations with our daughter about her body. Helping her take joy in the way God made her, along with using discretion in the clothes she wears, is a common theme in our house. It's difficult trying to talk about "sexy" clothes with a preteen, but she sees the ads and billboards just like everyone else. And we want to help her to know appropriate ways to respond to their messages.

A recent study concluded that 42 percent of all ten-to-seventeen-year-olds had viewed pornography on the Internet in the past year.[2] Another study said the average child's first exposure to Internet pornography is age eleven.[3] It would be foolish of me not to talk with my son about it in order to prepare him. The reality is that somewhere, sometime he will see pornography. When he does, I want him to know how to respond in a way that honors God and himself. I believe I would be setting him up for a moral defeat to do otherwise.

When it comes to life outside our home, we want to help our kids understand their responsibility to our community. I want them to respect the beauty and diversity of God's creation. I want them to understand their role in the melting pot of humanity. I want them to see the resilience and frailty of our environment and their responsibility to honor all that God has made. We want them to be pro-life in all aspects of their lives, so we teach the value of the unborn, the living, the elderly, and even those who practice a lifestyle we may disagree with.

As a blanket that covers all of life, we want them to know God deeply. We want them to see God as relevant to all aspects of their lives. He has created them each with a particular personality, a passion that continues to unfold, and values that are developed daily. We pray that they discover who God has made them to be and how to bring him glory through their lives.

For this kind of maturity and responsibility to develop, teens must have an honest understanding of the world. They must see both the beauty and the brokenness of life. They must come face-to-face with both the sacredness and sin of humanity. It's not easy to do, and there is no magic age in which certain experiences should happen or conversations should take place. And there is no guarantee that they will respond in a healthy way. But their best chance for honoring God with their choices is if you *guide them in making difficult choices now*, before they are forced to make them on their own. Like I said, it's a complex role parents play.

When teens succeed, we celebrate God's work in their lives. And when they fail, we celebrate God's work in their lives, because God is still at work. We grieve over their sin just as we do in our own lives. But we acknowledge that God is doing something. It is all a process. We prepare them so that in both failure and success, they see God's design for life.

More than Lines in the Sand

The only way for teens to experience this kind of completeness in character and health in life is to live within God's design for their lives, to live according to the way God meant for life to be best lived. Many choices may be good ones, but I'm not concerned with simply "good." Teens need to come face-to-face with what is God's "best." This requires boundaries.

I've heard people talk about having "clearly defined boundaries," or "healthy boundaries with others," or how we must "stay within biblical boundaries." While I would agree that the only way for our teens to experience the life that God truly intends is to stay within God's boundaries, I sometimes question how those boundaries are taught.

I remember growing up with the idea that God has drawn lines in the sand for *every possible situation* we might encounter. In my mind God was like a mean parent that stood over a young child with a hickory switch. He looks down at the youngster with narrowed eyes tapping the switch in his hand like a mean schoolteacher. He bends down, points the switch, and says, "Don't you even think about crossing that line." This seemed to fit the stories about God I was taught in my Sunday school classes. Stories of a couple thrown from a garden for eating the wrong fruit or a woman turned into a salt statue for looking the wrong way. And then there was the one of the family that was stoned for taking some gold from a fallen city. For some reason the details of these stories always stuck with me more than the stories of grace lived out by Jesus. Maybe it was because of the intensity with which they were told.

While the caricature may seem twisted, sadly it's not far from the kind of God many teens imagine. We have robbed them of a life of adventure, wonder, and amazement and replaced it with a list of do's and don'ts. *We*, not God, have boiled life down to acceptable and unacceptable behavior. God's boundaries are far less about rules than we make them.

Simply put, God's boundaries are his design for how life is supposed to work best. It is the Creator telling his creation how to function. Forgive the mechanistic overtones, but just as an inventor creates a machine with a particular function, purpose, or design, God has given us human beings a design, too.

As clearly as I can see, God's boundaries give us five aspects of our design. All five of these can be seen in his first interaction with Adam in the Book of Genesis. As you read about his encounter with God, take a few minutes and think about the words. What does it say to you about culture and your teen's life?

The LORD God took the man and put him in the Garden of Eden to work it and take care of it. And the LORD God commanded the man, "You are free to eat from any tree in the garden; but you must not eat from the tree of the knowledge of good and evil, for when you eat of it you will surely die." The LORD God said, "It is not good for the man to be alone. I will make a helper suitable for him." (Gen. 2:15–18, NIV)

God's Design Provides Direction

Our first observation is that God doesn't plop Adam down in the middle of this new paradise and say, "Okay. Go for it." From the moment Adam was formed, God was there giving him direction, showing him the lay of the land. Helping him understand his new home. Part of God's direction to Adam is the idea of responsible living. He expects Adam to take care of this garden. Keeping it cleaned and maintained is Adam's responsibility. God is communicating order and discipline. It's clear to Adam that he is responsible for his decisions and that his decisions will impact not just his own quality of life but the quality of life for the rest of creation.

Our teens need to understand that we are all responsible for our own actions. We have adopted a culture of blame in America, where everyone from McDonald's to Microsoft is found guilty for our addictions and poor health. Instead, we must teach personal responsibility. A responsibility that causes us to consider the effects of our decisions on ourselves, others around us, and the rest of creation.

This generation of teens has embraced new responsibilities. They should be commended for their attention to social-justice causes like poverty, racial reconciliation, fair trade, and home-lessness. These, and many other issues, are causes our generation failed in but resonate with this generation. In a recent study 82 percent of guys and 85 percent of girls said the environment was an important issue among their peers. They aren't just saying issues are important. They are actually doing something about it. Sixty-four percent of guys and 72 percent of girls said community service was important to them.[4] In helping our teens see their "whole self," we can demonstrate to them that being responsible in more personal areas—like spirituality, school, and family matters—will position them for greater success in facing the responsibilities of social causes they are drawn to.

God's Design Gives Freedom

The second truth we draw from this Genesis story is that life was not made to be a restrictive experience. From the very beginning God tells Adam that he is free to eat of anything he wants in the garden. He tells him to go and experience the abundance and fullness of all God has made. This garden was enormous, and it was Adam's own playground to explore.

This is similar to the picture Jesus paints for us of what a relationship with him is like. He says, "Yes, I am the gate. Those who come in through me will be saved. They will come and go freely and will find good pastures. The thief's purpose is to steal and kill and destroy. My purpose is to give them a rich and satisfying life" (John 10:9–10).

Jesus compares himself to the gate of a sheep pasture. There was only one gate that allowed the sheep into the pasture. Once inside, the sheep were allowed to romp and eat wherever they wanted. He doesn't say, "You come to me, and I'll put you on a chain and that's all the freedom you'll get." Instead, Jesus opens life up. He offers a fullness that can be experienced only within his design for us.

Imagine saying to your teen, "You are free to go and do whatever you want . . . within God's design." That's exactly what Jesus

169

says. Don't misunderstand; with freedom comes responsibility. But don't let your teens miss the freedom by overstating the boundaries.

God's Design Brings Protection

No, I didn't overlook it. There is one thing God told Adam to stay away from—a particular tree whose fruit would give Adam an experience he was not meant to bear. A knowledge he wouldn't be able to process.

Yes, God gives a prohibition to Adam, as he does to us. The question is, why? Notice God doesn't say, "Don't eat that, because I'll be mad at you." He tells Adam that if he chooses to eat from the tree, it will lead to his death. God is trying to protect Adam from something he was not designed to experience.

Our hearts don't know what to do with sin. We experience shame and isolation that we don't know how to handle. In fact, our instinctive response takes us further away from the protection we were designed to enjoy. As long as the sheep stays within the sheep pasture under the watchful eye of "the good shepherd," there is freedom and safety. When it ventures out on its own, there is no guarantee of protection.

Let's say your ninth-grade daughter comes bounding through the door and wants you to share her excitement about what happened today. She's all giddy because a senior boy came up to her at school and invited her to a party at a friend's house after the football game Friday night. After sharing this great news, she looks at you wide-eyed and says, "Well, Mom, can I go? Please. Please. Please."

The words on the tip of your tongue are probably something along the lines of, "You have lost your mind if you think I'm about to let you go to that party." In her mind this is a great opportunity, but you are wise enough to know otherwise. You know that if you allow her to go, you may be setting her up to make moral decisions under great pressure from peers that she may not be ready to make. She would be forced to navigate those waters alone, without your protection.

One time a boy in our neighborhood invited our son to a sleepover before we had a chance to meet his parents. We struggled between protecting our son and encouraging him in his friendships. We didn't want to deny him the joy of an invitation from a new friend, but we also needed to act responsibly.

It's these kinds of situations that have to be handled in such a way that your teen is able to experience freedom to pursue relationships but sees your protection as part of God's design. When God prompts us to says "no" or "wait" to something, it is not because he doesn't trust us. It's because it is not part of his best for us.

God's Design Ensures Healthy Relationships

Another observation is that from Adam's first encounter with God, we see that man was made for relationships both with God and with other people. I wish it were possible to know how Adam's relationship with God (or Eve) was different from ours. Since sin wasn't in the picture at first, there had to an amazing sense of vulnerability and transparency. There would be no reason to hide or pretend. Honesty and honor would define the relationship. Even though sin is now part of our baggage, through our redemption, God equips us to live again with honesty and vulnerability.

Adolescence is the most transforming and troubling time in life. Everything in a teen's life seems to change overnight. And it continues to change for a few years. During this time teens are grasping for anything that is consistent and stable. For most teens, the most precarious parts of the whole experience are their relationships, particularly with adults. It's hard for teens to know whom they can trust. There are people at school or church they would call friends, but they still keep a watchful eye on those "friends," because they've been burned too many times. Even healthy overtures of friendship by adults are met with skepticism. Too many teachers, pastors, parents, and coaches have moved in and out of their lives already. They feel disillusioned about the hope of a healthy relationship with anyone.

The only way for the pattern of distrust and self-protection to be broken is for a teenager to meet a God who loves them completely and perfectly. His design offers a relationship with himself unlike anything they have ever experienced.

Besides your home, the best place for your teen to understand how God receives them is in a spiritual community with peers, particularly while in middle school. Church youth programs can offer teens healthy relationships with other adults and peers and help them get grounded in their faith before the bigger pressures of high school come up. There are also many faith-based programs in schools (Young Life, FCA, First Priority, etc.) that do a great job getting students connected in meaningful spiritually based relationships and activities.[5]

God's Design Maintains Authority

Think of this final aspect of God's design as a blanket that covers everything else. From the beginning, God designed us to live under authority regardless of our age or position. Jesus even models this for us when he tells us, "I tell you the truth, the Son can do nothing by himself. He does only what he sees the Father doing. Whatever the Father does, the Son also does" (John 5:19). Jesus is not a cavalier leader blazing his own trail. He lives in submission to the Father and his plan.

The Designer has ultimate authority over the design. It's only when we try to take authority into our own hands that things go wrong, just as they did for Adam. When I immigrate to another country, I lose all the rights and privileges that come with being an American citizen. In the same way, when I step outside of God's authority, I lose all freedom of adventure and fullness, I'm no longer under his protection from sin, and I forfeit healthy relationships.

When I approach life from God's design, I can answer my teen's questions of moral choices in a whole new way. It doesn't have to be about me and what makes me comfortable. Or about me trying to remember all the things I did wrong when I was a teen so I can be sure and tell my own kids to avoid those things. Instead, I can point them toward God's design. I can help them see what he says is for their best.

When I was a youth pastor, the number one question I was asked by teens had nothing to do with God or heaven or salvation. The question was, "How far is too far?" As in, "How much can my girlfriend and I fool around and it not be a sin?" Honestly, I can't remember many camps where the topic didn't come up during guys' cabin time.

I always found the question curious, because even the youngest of teens were trying to figure out where the "line in the sand" was. Yes, God does have a clear boundary when it comes to sex before marriage, but I don't think that's what teens are getting at when asking the question. They want to maximize their pleasure without the guilt from sin. Or at least that's what I was trying to do when I was in high school.

I remember feeling pressure as a young pastor to have just the right words to answer their questions. I didn't realize until many years later what a poor question it is. The real question should be, "What is God's design for me sexually?" Followed by deeper questions: Will this choice bring honor to you or the other person? Do you feel a sense of freedom in your decision or a need to hide it from others? Are you looking out for the best interest of the other person when you make your choice? These kinds of questions help teens begin to think critically about God's boundaries for life, allowing them to draw conclusions they can own for themselves.

In the end, I'm not trying to come up with all the right words to say, so much as the right questions to ask. And regardless of the situation, the basic question never changes—what is God's design? It's not about avoiding a line in the sand or keeping a list of rules. It's about me helping my kids understand what God's design is for their lives.

Do you remember the most recent moral conversation (or confrontation) you had with your teens? Did you simply give them the perfect rebuttal as to why the choice was wrong, or did you help them think through the situation so they can choose what is best the next time? Stop for a moment and think of a constructive question you could ask—a question that helps them think critically about their choice.

In a Land Far, Far Away

In biblical times, Daniel was a teenager who understood God's design for life. He knew how to be part of his culture and still fully live out his faith. He knew how to be in community with others who were not like him. He showed respect for those in authority over him, even when he was told to do something he couldn't go along with.

Daniel came from a respectable family in Judah. He was intelligent, attractive, and physically fit. By any culture's teen standards, Daniel had everything going for him. But there was one aspect of Daniel's life we aren't told much about, and yet we know it's what really defined him. His faith and spiritual disciplines set him apart from the rest of the royal subjects of his day.

At some point in Daniel's early teen years, his country was ravaged and plundered by the Babylonians. Overnight, his life was changed forever. Physique, intellect, and beauty were prized by the Babylonian king, so Daniel and other young men like him were taken as a special prize. I can't imagine the fear raging inside these young men as they were ripped from their homes, watched as their parents were killed or taken as slaves, and then marched 700 miles away into a land they had never seen. Most of these men, including Daniel, would never see Judah again.

From then on, the culture and ways of the Babylonians would become Daniel's culture too. It would have had to have been a time of complete culture shock for any Israelite. No more family. No more protection. No more king. And their place of worship, the temple, had been destroyed, replaced by gold and bronze statues of pagan gods. A kingdom of excess and power would be their new home for the next seventy years.

Put yourself in Daniel's shoes. You are fifteen years old and see temple prostitutes for the first time. Standing on every corner are women offering sexual favors for a pagan god's appeasement. Outside the king's temple are scantily clad women and giant statues to gods you've never heard of. You see and hear things you never knew existed. At first it's shocking and overwhelming. But then you stop to think about it. A whole new world has been opened up to you, and it's ripe for the picking. Anything goes. There are no taboos. No one to tell you no. None of the boundaries God gave regarding sex, work ethic, diet, commerce, or possessions apply in this land.

Daniel had to choose how to respond to the challenges of this new culture. He could have chosen to be resentful and angry at the corruption of power that surrounded him. He could have chosen to isolate himself from the sin and decadence of the Babylonian culture. Maybe even band together a few friends to try and escape or seek holy revenge against evil by killing some of their captors. Instead, Daniel made the choice to fully engage the culture he found himself part of and still remain true to his Hebrew heritage and teachings. For Daniel, it was not an issue of *if* he would be part of this new world. It was the *only way* he could be an influence for justice, change, and truth.

Daniel was able to move toward this goal because he understood God's design. God's boundaries allowed him to love and respect others without compromising truth. I've read his story over and over again and never cease to be amazed at the maturity and presence of mind this young teen shows under pressure.

Daniel made lifestyle choices that to some of his Hebrew counterparts may have seemed like compromise or "being of the world." I'm sure Daniel was aware of the glances and whispers of some of the fundamentalists of his day. Perhaps he was the scorn of those who would think, "We may be the Babylonians' slaves, but I'm not going to have anything to do with their culture." I'm sure there were some, as in our own day, whose rationale was, "We are aliens and strangers here. This place is not our home. We are destined for a much better place, so why get involved?"

Daniel never practiced this kind of detached behavior. He lived out a greater plan. A more balanced approach. This was an opportunity, as Beth Moore says, "to become culturally relevant without becoming spiritually irrelevant."[6]

The Babylonian culture valued knowledge as much as Daniel did, and he learned "the language and literature of Babylon."[7] For three years he learned everything an educated Babylonian would have learned. He studied history, astronomy, mathematics, art, and medicine. I'm sure no parent would have a problem with any of these disciplines. But what of the other areas the Babylonians studied: incantation, exorcism, divination by dreams, and astrology? Daniel would have studied all of these as well. Don't misread this. I'm not saying Daniel practiced any of these things. What I am saying is that Daniel would have had a working knowledge of these practices and how each fit into the Babylonian culture.

It's easy to see why Daniel was consulted when the king had trouble with a dream. From a human perspective, Daniel understood all the nuances of what the king was looking for in an answer to his dream. He knew how to relate to the king because he had studied divination. But God gave him an "unusual aptitude for understanding every aspect of literature and wisdom" and a "special ability to interpret the meanings of visions and dreams." In other words, because of the Babylonians' fascination with dreams, God entrusted to Daniel a unique ability to understand them. God knew this gift would place Daniel in a prestigious position in the Babylonian culture. When comparing all the magicians in the kingdom, the king found Daniel and his friends to be ten times more reliable.

Early on, when a situation arose in which Daniel felt he was being asked to cross a personal spiritual boundary, he handled it with maturity and tact. The king ordered that all his trainees be fed the same choice meats and wine that he himself would eat. He wanted these men to be the most physically fit of any in his kingdom. Probably because of Hebrew dietary laws, Daniel and his three friends felt it would be a moral compromise to eat the king's food. The king had given a directive, but Daniel "determined not to defile himself." Again, Daniel is probably around age fifteen. How would you have handled this kind of pressure at fifteen? Better yet, by watching and listening to you, how has your teenager learned to handle this kind of social pressure?

Daniel and the others could have started a picket march, carrying signs that read, "Choose fruit. Not meat!" They could have written condemning letters to the king. They could have prayed for God's judgment against such injustice. Thankfully, Daniel had more maturity than many of our contemporaries. We are told that God had given the chief official great respect for Daniel. That kind of relationship doesn't happen overnight. Daniel treated those in authority over him with respect. He was gracious even in his captivity. He asked his guard to reconsider and test them for ten days to see what God might do. He didn't put his foot down or make demands. He asked for permission.

Several years later, the king orders the death of all the magicians because of their inability to recall and interpret the king's dream. Daniel goes to the commander with "wisdom and discretion" to ask for one more day to seek the answer. After getting the answer from God, Daniel goes before the king in humility and tells him, "It is not because I am wiser than any one else that I know the secret of your dream." He goes on to tell him that the only reason that he knows about the king's dream is because the God he worships has revealed it to him. After interpreting the dream, the king declares Daniel's God as the God of gods.

Daniel's actions didn't just save his life. The lives of all the pagan magicians were spared as well. Because of the choices Daniel made, the king had an encounter with Daniel's God, and an unjust command was rescinded. Daniel was made ruler over the province of Babylon, and the king placed Daniel's friends in charge of his personal affairs. Not bad for a day's work.

At any point during these years, Daniel could have said, "That's it. This place is corrupt and beyond redeeming. It's just not worth it." He could have refused to obey, chosen death, or distanced himself and tried to blend in with everyone else.

You don't "find favor" with the king by remaining distant or condemning. Instead, Daniel engaged the culture around him, and God was glorified.

Perhaps it was Daniel's example the apostle Paul drew from when he spoke to Athenians about their altar to an "unknown god." Because he understood Roman culture and gods, he was able to use this as an opportunity to share the truth of Christ. He gave their unknown god a name—Jesus. He didn't point out the flaws in their worship. Instead, he focused his energies on "sharing the truth in love," as he later tells us to do.

No Fear of Bunnies

Sometimes I imagine how my kids would respond if they were in situations similar to Daniel's. And then I remind myself that they already are. They regularly encounter modern-day Babylonians, who use advertising to exploit sexuality for financial profit. They hear messages that more stuff is what brings happiness—more CDs, newer video games, just the right clothes, and so on. Their world of entertainment conveys a consistent message that authority figures like parents, teachers, and pastors are inept and irrelevant. These are similar to the experiences Daniel had to deal with.

It would be easy to feel defeated. But I don't. Instead of being distracted by the dysfunction and sin of our world, I focus on God's redemption at work in my family. I prepare my kids to live in the world by understanding God's design for life and helping them see the joy and fullness that comes in living within that design. They see the brokenness of their world but are still drawn to love the people in it.

I don't live in fear of Hugh Hefner, MTV, or countless Hollywood studios. Instead, I hurt for them and the emptiness of their invitation. The only hope for a better message to be heard in our world is if families begin to fill in the culture's cracks with the love and mercy of God.

I pray that God would allow your family to move into your culture in such a way that the light and love of Christ transforms the lives of those around you. I pray that our children would be able to show others a different way of living in community and how to experience healthy and whole relationships. I pray that their footsteps would leave behind both grace and truth. I pray the broken and hurting would find a place of refuge in your home and leave your doors having met the one who made them.

When "I Don't Know" Is the Only Honest Answer

[Teens] want people who will sit with them and talk about the big questions, even if they don't know the answers; adults who won't correct their feelings and pretend not to be afraid.

Anne Lamott[1]

More often than I like to admit, I have the same uncomfortable moment when I'm in conversations with others. It happens with family, friends, and total strangers. The conversation is going well. The topic is interesting. There is a mutual give-and-take of dialogue. We're rolling along in a deep conversation about European politics, the theological concept of redemption, God's views on social justice, or Apple computers. And then it happens.

Even though I hear words coming from my mouth, I know the conversation has gone beyond my knowledge of the subject. I hear a frustrated voice in my head saying, "Just shut up!" Yet I continue to speak.

I'm not quite sure why. Maybe I'm afraid the other person will catch on that I don't know what I'm talking about. So instead of being quiet, I conjecture or ramble. I'm pretty sure this behavior would fit somewhere in Solomon's definition of a fool.

Another reason might be I'm afraid to say, "I don't know." In my role as a pastor or "culture expert" (whatever that means), I can think of times someone asked me a question because they thought I would know the answer. They pose the question, then stare at me with that "please help" look. It's so easy in those moments to put pressure on myself to have just the right words of wisdom, as if I alone can provide what they need. This is nothing more than an inward idolatry.

These are the same traps I fall into with my family. When my wife starts a conversation with me by saying, "Why do you think . . . ," I find myself sticking out my chest, proud that she needs my wisdom. Or my son walks in the room and says, "Dad, can I talk to you for a minute about . . . ," and my mind starts racing to find the right words as if he will crumble under the weight of the world *right now* without my help.

It's easy to forget that since all truth originates in God, I have nothing original to say. These are his principles and wisdom—not mine. When I speak truth to my family, I am merely passing on what he has already declared is right, true, lovely, and worth talking about. But whenever I try and take credit for his words or promptings, I have elevated myself above the Creator, at least in my own heart.

If I could change only one thing in our culture, it wouldn't be the quality of shows on TV, or the violence in video games, or even pornography on the Internet. I would change me. I would want myself to be able to stop and listen to the Spirit's voice inside me that says, "Just be still. Be quiet. Let me reign in you. Listen to me."

There is an ancient Hebrew song that starts by saying, "In the morning, O LORD, you hear my voice; in the morning I lay my requests before you and wait in expectation" (Ps. 5:3, NIV). There is a posture of the heart in those words that I long for. Not so much in the first part—I do well enough telling God all the things I need help with. It's that last phrase I have trouble with . . . *and wait in expectation*. Those four words say, "I don't know what to do. I don't know the answer. You, O God, know what is right. I want you to tell me. And I'm not moving forward until I hear from you." Instead, I blow forward trying to lead or give an answer to my kids without first hearing from God.

Solomon pleaded with his own son to listen to his wisdom. He said, "O my son, give me your heart. May your eyes take delight in following my ways" (Prov. 23:26). Solomon is asking his son for trust. Trust that he knows what is best. Trust that he knows the way to go. It has absolutely nothing to do with what the son knows or his own experiences.

For me the word *delight* is the transformative word in the father's call. I'm learning there is a great freedom in saying, "I don't have a clue what to do, but I'm so glad God does." I feel I am taking my first steps as a parent toward delighting in his wisdom, and not in what I might think is right. I don't have to be enslaved to panic or fear because I can't think of just the right words for my family. Instead, I can delight in being the son of a good Father whose knowledge is limitless. I can delight in knowing that he will freely tell me what is right. I just need to be still long enough to hear. I can delight that his words can be trusted and acted on.

One day Mona and I were reminiscing about our relationship and all the things we've learned about each other. After laughing about silly things we did to try and impress each other while dating, I asked her when it was that she finally decided she could entrust her heart to me. She said, "After you took me for a walk in the park. Right then, in that moment, I knew."

I loved going on creative dates and doing things that were out of the ordinary. And those are the only kind of dates we went on. I remember our relationship getting to that fun place where we couldn't wait to learn as much as possible about each other. That time in a relationship where you sit and talk at a restaurant for hours and forget there is anyone else around. That's the kind of date we had the night she finally trusted me.

We went to a park late at night when no one else was around. We got out of my car and started walking across a field toward the swings. As Mona was sitting in the swing, I walked behind her and asked her to close her eyes. I said, "We're going to go for a walk, and I just want you to hold my arm as we walk."

Soon after we started walking, it began to lightly drizzle, which added an unexpected element to the experience. And as we walked, I quietly asked Mona questions about her life. What did she enjoy about college? What most surprised her about God? When was she most afraid? What was her favorite food?

Before we knew it, we had been walking more than an hour. Unbeknownst to me, with every question I asked and the longer we walked, she was entrusting her heart to me. Because her eyes were closed, she was no longer in control. She had no say in where we would go or in what would happen next. She felt a freedom to trust that I would not lead her into harm.

I wake up every day knowing that the world waiting for me will be different than it was yesterday. It feels confusing and disorienting, just like walking into the grocery store and realizing they moved everything around from the week before. The layout doesn't make sense, and I have to plot a different course to find what I need.

I wish life would slow down and be more predictable at times. Just when I think I've figured out what my kids need from me, they come up with something different. No matter how much studying I do, this "new course" in their lives doesn't make sense. My own knowledge and experiences fall short of the answers. I feel myself grasping, aching to find the right words or do the right thing. Then, at the height of my tension, I hear his voice again . . . "Be still. Just be quiet. Let me have your heart. Trust in my wisdom."

Freedom. Release. Deep breath.

In those moments, it is no longer about my need to engage my teenager's world. It is about letting my Creator engage my heart.

Group Discussion Guide

Introduction

There is a tendency in group book discussions to get a few people together and spend all the time talking about where you agreed and disagreed with the author. Let that be only part of your discussion. Move past the stories in the book to your own experiences. Respond from what you know to be true.

The following questions are for you to think through alone or with a small group of other parents. They are meant primarily to be conversation starters. Don't let them be the end of your thinking on the subject. Let the Holy Spirit guide the conversation as you discuss each topic.

If you are leading a group discussion, take some time to ready yourself. Think of a story from your own experience as a parent, one that ties in with the chapter topic. Think through how you would respond to each of the questions.

Chapter One—Fear

1. Think this through:
   I would say that the part of my daughter's/son's culture that has the most influence on him/her right now is _____ (movies/television, friends, dating, violence, alcohol/drugs, wealth/possessions, status/popularity, family, other).
2. Finish this thought:
   I experience fear when I think of my child at _____ (school, home alone, a certain friend's house, the computer, boyfriend/girlfriend's car). Why at this place? How much of this is rational, and how much irrational?
3. What is it you most want to protect your child from (getting hurt, experiencing ridicule, facing consequences of poor choices, acting outside your area of wisdom, other)?
4. Read 2 Timothy 1:7. Paul is talking to Timothy about his tendency toward fear in relationships, particularly in speaking the truth. How might you respond to your teen's culture with the spirit of power, love, and self-discipline that God has given you?
5. Try to remember a time you effectively responded to a crisis situation without fear. What happened?

Chapter Two—Isolation

1. Think this through:
   What is one area of my child's culture in which I can see genuine goodness and can support wholeheartedly (music, movie, friendship, sports hero, celebrity)?
2. Finish this thought:

I tend to want to build a moat around my child when it comes to _____.

3. We all build moats around our lives, to some extent. What about the moat-building model do you see as a downfall in raising your child?

4. There is much in our culture that makes it easy to want to scream and begin digging a trench. Think about each of these issues and how you can address them with your teenager instead of barricading yourself from them.
   —Sexuality in media
   —Lifestyle of excess
   —Disregard of authority
   —Unhealthy choices

Chapter Three—Blame

1. Think this through:
   When your son/daughter has an uncharacteristically bad attitude, whom do you tend to blame (TV character, friend, music, celebrity, your child, other)?

2. Finish this thought:
   Of the first three ways of responding to culture discussed in chapters 1–3, the way I most often instinctively tend to respond is _____ (fear, building a moat, blame). Why?

3. Look at the newspaper headlines on page 47. What other things have you seen parents blame for teenagers' behavior?

4. Sometimes as parents, we defend our kids because we don't want to admit our responsibility in the matter, or we look at them through rose-colored glasses. If you were to fall into one of these two traps, which would it be? Why?

5. When you choose to blame the world for problems, what begins to happen to your heart toward the world?

Chapter Four—Ignorance

1. Think this through:
   What things in your teen's life do you honestly feel ignorant about (Internet, school issues, current dating and relationships, free time interests, spiritual growth, other)?
2. This one is a little harder. In which areas of your teen's life do you wear blinders, even if slightly, because you are afraid to fully know what might be there?
3. The author comments, "A feeling of being unequipped or inadequate keep parents from acting." In which areas of your teen's life do you feel inadequate?
4. Look at the four truths listed on page 59. Which of these do you really need to believe right now? What does the statement mean to you? How can you live out this truth today?
5. Finish this thought:
   I am going to look for opportunities to bring up the subject of _____ with my child.

Chapter Five—Influence

1. Think this through:
   When you see the pie chart of influences in your teen's life, which area gives you the most concern (media, peers, school, law, parents)? Why?
2. Read the first paragraph on page 63 again. How can you begin to "change for the better" each of these areas in

your teen's life: Internet habits, choices in friends, media influences, school activities?

3. How has God redeemed unhealthy influences in your own life over the years? How can you use your own experiences to redemptively influence areas of your teen's life?

4. Read over these verses and consider what the application of each may be as you move into different areas of your teen's life:

Ephesians 2:10, Ephesians 2:12–13, Ephesians 4:2, Ephesians 6:16.

5. Finish this thought:

If I rearrange a few things in my own life, I can begin to "ooze" over into my teen's life in the area of _____.

Chapter Six—Values

1. Think this through:

When you consider the things your teen focuses time and energy on, what values do you see revealed?

2. Look at the Behavior/Value chart on page 77. When have you recently seen your teen have a good value that was poorly executed? How did you respond in that situation?

3. Do you spend more of your time focused on the actions of your teen or on the values being pursued by those actions? Why?

4. Read Romans 12:1–2. Rank from 1–10 (10 being highest). When it comes to "being good," would you say your teen:

_____ Conforms to the behavior of his or her peers.

_____ Conforms to what you say is good.

_____ Is transformed by God at work in him or her.

5. How can you direct your teen's attention toward God as the one who can fully meet his or her needs?

6. Finish these thoughts:
   I can help meet my son's/daughter's need for . . .
   Authenticity by _____.
   Security by _____.
   Community by _____.
   Affirmation by _____.

Chapter Seven—Transitions

1. Think this through:
   Review the questions on page 100. Based on the age of your teen, do you think your parenting style should be more authoritative or more relational at this point?

2. Which type of influence comes most naturally to you? How do you balance being both a relational and an authoritative influence with your teen? How might you need to be more of one than the other?

3. Read the quotes from Christian Smith on page 104 How do you see yourself influencing your teen's religious choices? How do you walk with your teen through his or her spiritual journey?

4. Look at the charts on page 102. How does this hit you? If your teen was asked to rank the question, "I have a good relationship with my mom/dad," what would they point to on the chart? Explain.

5. Finish this thought:
   As my child grows older, I see my relationship with him or her becoming more _____.

Chapter Eight—Passion

1. Think this through:
   When your teen talks about his or her future, what topics really get him or her going? What does your teen currently have a passion for?
2. Do you find yourself more likely to (a) try to protect your teen from making mistakes, or (b) open the world up for exploration? How can you begin to say "yes" to your teen's passions?
3. If someone wrote a story about your life, what kind of story would it be (romance, tragedy, comedy, etc.)? What kind of story would your teen want his or her life to be?
4. Read Philippians 3:8. How do you model for your child a willingness to die to all else in order to passionately live for God's glory? How might your teen's values and passion come into play in helping him or live out this verse?
5. Finish this thought:
   I can begin to be involved in my teen's area of interest and/or passion by _____.

Chapter Nine—Design

1. Think this through:
   What is one area of life in which your teen feels pressured to be like you?
2. What ways has God wired your teen that are unique to him or her (personality strengths, talents, aptitudes, learning styles, etc.)?
3. Proverbs 22:6 talks about raising a child according to the way God has made him or her. If you have multiple

children, how might you need to teach them "according to their way"?

4. How does the way God made you and the way he made your teen cause conflict at times? How can you resolve the conflict in such a way that still affirms how God has made you each to approach life?

5. Finish this thought (aloud or in a note to your teen): Do you know what I like most about the way God has made you? I love it that you are _____. Explain.

Chapter Ten—Community

1. Think this through:
   What does real community look like to you? Would your teen say that your family experiences community in your neighborhood? Why or why not?

2. A quote from page 140 reads, "If we do not first love, then we cannot expect to be heard." How does this meld with your own attempts to share your faith?

3. Think about the story of the man on the Harley who came to the neighborhood cookout. Can you think of a time when you experienced a conflict of values between you and a neighbor? How did you respond?

4. Look at the list on page 147 of ways to engage your community and neighbors. Which one of these jumps out at you as something that your family could do?

5. Finish this thought:
   Our family is trying to live out the love of Christ to our neighbors by _____.

Chapter Eleven—Redemption

1. Think this through:
   The metaphor of a river was used to describe culture. In the way you live around others in the world are you more like:
   a. Chad Pregracke and trying to clean up the culture;
   b. the families who put up the orange barricade to keep the pollution away; or
   c. those who dig their own "Christian" river that runs parallel to that of the culture?

2. Read the quote from John Stott on page 154. He says there are two responses we have toward the world: escape or engage. Describe what each of these looks like. What is the attraction toward each of these?

3. Eli Morris said, "When you are geographically removed from the poor, you become emotionally removed from them as well." What other people in our culture are forgotten because of your distance from them? Which of these are by choice, and which are circumstantial?

2. Finish this thought:
   _____ is one way I choose to engage those around me.

Chapter Twelve—Boundaries

1. Think this through:
   Teens' best chance of honoring God with their choices is if you guide them in making difficult choices before they are forced to make them on their own. How are you preparing your teen to walk responsibly in the culture he or she is a part of? How do you help your teen think through choices?

2. When your teen has a moral failure, how do you help him or her through the guilt, grieving, and restoration process?

3. There are five different aspects to God's boundaries. How do you live out each of these in your family?

   a. Boundaries provide direction.

   b. Boundaries give freedom.

   c. Boundaries bring protection.

   d. Boundaries ensure healthy relationships.

   e. Boundaries maintain authority.

4. Your teen asks permission to go to a party at a friend's house. "Everybody from school" will be there. There will be no parents around. How can you explain your answer in light of the five aspects of God's boundaries?

5. How does Daniel move toward those in his culture instead of running from them? How can Daniel's story be an example for your own teenager?

Chapter Thirteen—Trust

1. Read this verse from Psalm 5:3 again. "In the morning, O LORD, you hear my voice. In the morning I lay my requests before you and wait in expectation" (NIV). What does it mean to you to "wait in expectation"? Why is waiting so difficult? In those moments when waiting for God's prompting or voice becomes too unbearable, how do you find yourself responding?

2. Most of us respond to situations in our own strength and knowledge. We miss the joy of being led by God and being moved by his words. What steps do you take in your life to make waiting and listening for God a normal part of your experience?

3. Take some time this month to try one of the following exercises. There is nothing magical about any of them. It's not really the exercise that is important. Instead, the goal is positioning your mind and heart in such a way that God can break through the noise of your life. In each of these suggestions, take time to ask God to slow your thoughts, calm your heart, and enable you to hear him speak.

   a. Sit on your back porch quietly sipping a cup of coffee or tea until your cup is empty. Tell God what is on your mind after every sip. Pay attention to any verses or direction he might bring to mind.

   b. Stare out your front window with all the media turned off. Talk to God about whatever comes to mind. Then turn on a favorite worship song and let God calm your heart as you focus on the lyrics to the song.

   c. Go to a park and sit under a tree on a blanket. Let God direct your thoughts as you observe your surroundings.

   d. Fill a blank piece of paper with your thoughts to God first thing in the morning. Do it again as the last thing at night. Compare the differences in your two pages.

4. Think of a time your teen asked you a question that you were afraid to answer or didn't know the answer. How did you respond? How did you wish you could have responded? How could you have "waited" to respond?

5. After all you've read, what are two or three things you've taken away from this book? How has applying some of these principles made a difference in your relationship with your teen?

The Conversation Continues

If you have been meeting with a group to work through these questions, there is no reason to stop just because the book is finished. In talking to others, hopefully one of the things you've learned is that every parent is struggling to relate to and lead their teens. You are not alone. I encourage you to be an advocate for one another. Continue the conversation that has started through this study. Decide to meet together—if not as a whole then at least with a few—and share questions and stories that continue to come up as you walk through this journey of adolescence with your teens. For further discussion, there are many parenting articles available at www.awaketolife.org, or you can feel free to include Brian in your discussion by emailing comments or questions to brian@awaketolife.org.

Notes

Introduction

1. Robert Lewis with Rob Wilkins, *The Church of Irresistible Influence* (Grand Rapids: Zondervan, 2001), 40.

2. *NBC Nightly News*, video podcast, October 1, 2007, MSNBC.com.

3. Tony Campolo, *Partly Right: Christianity Responds to Its Critics* (Dallas: Word, 1985), 35.

4. Ibid., 36.

Chapter 1

1. André Gide, en.wikiquote.org/wiki/Andr%C3%A9_Gide.

2. Aletha C. Huston, Edward Donnerstein, Halford Fairchild, et al. *Big World, Small Screen: The Role of Television in American Society* (Lincoln: University of Nebraska Press, 1992).

Chapter 2

1. Quote Garden, www.quotegarden.com/fear.html.

2. Spencer Burke, *A Heretic's Guide to Eternity* (San Francisco: Jossey-Bass, 2006), 92.

3. Derek Webb, "Standing Up for Nothing," *Caedmon's Call*, Cumbee Road Music, ASCAP, 1997.

4. H. Richard Niebuhr, *Christ and Culture* (San Francisco: HarperSanFrancisco, 1951), 213.

5. Rob Bell, *Velvet Elvis* (Grand Rapids: Zondervan, 2005), 82.

6. Burke, *Heretic's Guide*, 213.

7. For more on the efforts of Live Earth, visit www.liveearth.org.

Chapter 3

1. Think Exist.com, http://thinkexist.com/quotes/rainer_maria_rilke.
2. The Quotations Page, www.quotationspage.com/quote/1081.html.
3. Britney Spears, ". . . Baby One More Time," *Britney Spears Greatest Hits: My Prerogative*, Zamba Recording LLC, 2005.
4. Alice Peacock, "I'll Start with Me," *Alice Peacock*, 2002, EMI April Music. Used with permission.

Chapter 4

1. Think Exist.com, http://thinkexist.com/quotes/frank_zappa.
2. The Quotations Page, www.quotationspage.com/quote/34043.html.
3. Overall, 44.9 percent of high school students reported drinking alcohol during the past thirty days (28.8 percent binge-drank and 16.1% drank alcohol but did not binge-drink). "Binge Drinking and Associated Health Risk Behaviors Among High School Students," in *Pediatrics*, 119, no. 1 (Jan. 2007).
4. This was scribbled on scrap paper during one of my meetings with Steve Collums in his office.
5. Justin McRoberts, "Trust You," *Trust*, Five Foot Six and a Half Music, 2002. Used with permission.

Chapter 5

1. Brian D. McLaren, *A New Kind of Christian* (San Francisco: Jossey-Bass, 2001), 75.
2. Walter A. Elwell, ed., *Baker Encyclopedia of the Bible*, vol. 2 (Grand Rapids: Baker, 1988).
3. *Webster's Ninth New Collegiate Dictionary* (Springfield, MA: Merriam-Webster, 1987).
4. This pie chart of influences is merely anecdotal and not scientific. Not every teen's pie will look exactly alike.
5. Thanks to Chris Pekary for the nachos and great discussion on parenting. I don't know if I would have been able to take an honest look at myself if it were not for your candor and questions.

Chapter 6

1. Chap Clark, *Hurt* (Grand Rapids: Baker Academic, 2004), 145.
2. Thanks to Brian Briley for every story you've ever shared with me. They leave me longing more for the Christ who lives in you. I've never had a friend who makes me feel as valued as you.
3. Thanks to Tobias Simers for the countless phone conversations and for making it snow in St. Louis. You are the most transparent friend I've ever known. I can't thank you enough for both your hard questions and the mercy you extend regardless of whether my answers are tempered or raw.
4. Peter Scazzero, *The Emotionally Healthy Church* (Grand Rapids: Zondervan, 2003).

5. Clark, *Hurt*, 43.

6. Jeff Grabmeier, "Parents Can Help Teens Choose 'Good' Friends, Study Finds," Ohio State Research, http://researchnews.osu.edu/archive/adolfrnd.htm.

7. James Garbarino, *Lost Boys: Why Our Sons Turn Violent and How We Can Save Them* (New York: Free Press, 1999).

8. This concept is borrowed from Dr. Gary Chapman. He has written a series of books on relationships, the original being *The Five Love Languages*.

9. Patricia Hersch, *A Tribe Apart* (New York: Ballantine, 2000), 13.

Chapter 7

1. BrainyQuote, http://www.brainyquote.com/quotes/quotes/b/billcosby156772.html.

2. QuoteWorld.org, http://www.quoteworld.org/quotes/1544.

3. Josh McDowell and Bob Hostetler, *Right from Wrong* (Dallas: Word, 1994), 284–85.

4. Ibid., 284–90.

5. Thanks to Chap Clark for your wisdom and e-mail correspondences for this book. Thousands of youth pastors are indebted to your research.

6. Christian Smith with Melinda Lundquist Denton, *Soul Searching: The Religious and Spiritual Lives of American Teenagers* (New York: Oxford University Press, 2005), 56.

7. Ibid., 56.

8. Judith Wallerstein, Julia M. Lewis, and Sandra Blakeslee, *The Unexpected Legacy of Divorce: A 25 Year Landmark Study* (New York: Hyperion, 2000), 32.

Chapter 8

1. Think Exist.com, http://thinkexist.com/quotation/those_who_danced_were_thought_to_be_quite_insane/163224.html.

2. Quoted from *Braveheart*, dir. Mel Gibson, Icon Productions, 1995 B.H. Finance C.V., ARR.

3. Think Exist.com, http://thinkexist.com/quotation/passion-it-lies-in-all-of-us-sleeping-waiting/411216.html.

4. Donald Miller was a speaker at the Orange Conference, May 2007, Atlanta, GA. His message on life as a story challenged me to think of my life in a whole new way.

5. I'm not exactly sure when he said or if it was ever in print. The book of Young Life's official history is also entitled *It's a Sin to Bore a Kid*.

6. Tony Campolo, *You Can Make a Difference* (Dallas: Word Publishing, 1984).

7. Shane Claiborne, *The Irresistible Revolution: Living as an Ordinary Radical* (Grand Rapids, Zondervan, 2006), 202.

8. See www.hoopsofhope.org to read Aaron's story.

9. Francine Rivers, *A Voice in the Wind* (Carol Stream, IL: Tyndale, 1993).

10 Keynote address by Louie Giglio at the Passion Conference, January 2000, Dallas, TX.

11. Think Exist.com, http://thinkexist.com/quotation/the-way-you-get-meaning-into-your-life-is-to/386876.html.

Chapter 9

1. Jessica Andrews, "Who I Am," *Who I Am*, UMG Recordings, 2001.
2. Definitely one of the greatest movies ever. *The Breakfast Club*, DVD, directed by John Hughes (Hollywood: Universal City Studios, 1985).
3. This is one of the most common interpretations of this phrase. Another is "according to the way a child should be raised."
4. If you take a family trip to Branson, it's well worth it to go see Kirby. His show is a great example of sharing your faith in the culture you are part of. You'll have to see the show to understand. Go to www.kirbyvanburch.com.

Chapter 10

1. Donald Miller, *Blue like Jazz* (Nashville: Thomas Nelson, 2003), 218.
2. Ibid., 220.
3. There are many films that address social issues that every Christian should have a response to. Here are a few of the films that give a fuller meaning to the term "pro-life." Not all are suitable for a younger audience: *Freedom Writer, The Invisible Children, Crash, Hotel Rwanda, An Inconvenient Truth, Bella, Big Ideas for a Small Planet.*
4. Organizations like Habitat for Humanity and Samaritan's Purse are great places to start.
5. Youth Serve America partners with thousands of community service groups in America to give teenagers a place to serve (www.ysa.org).

Chapter 11

1. Wisdom Quotes, http://www.wisdomquotes.com/000154.html.
2. John Galvin, "Dude over Troubled Water," *Outside Magazine*, August 2002.
3. www.livinglandsandwaters.org.
4. Rick Rusaw and Eric Swanson, *The Externally Focused Church* (Loveland, CO: Group, 2004), 41.
5. John Stott, *Involvement: Being a Responsible Christian in a Non-Christian Society* (Old Tappan, NJ: Fleming H. Revell, 1984), 34.
6. Mark Driscoll, *The Church Creating Culture*. 2006 Desiring God Conference podcast, Desiring God Ministries.
7. Thanks to Eli Morris for his transparency and authenticity. I love the way you are willing to walk into different parts of our culture to take God's redeeming love.
8. Stott, *Involvement*, 35.

Chapter 12

1. Tony Campolo, *Growing Up in America* (Grand Rapids: Zondervan, 1989), 20.

2. Janis Wolak, Kimberly Mitchell, and David Finkelhor, "Unwanted and Wanted Exposure to Online Pornography in a National Sample of Youth Internet Users," *Pediatrics* 119 (2007), 247–57.

3. TopTenREVIEWS, www.internet-filter-review.toptenreviews.com.

4. *The TRU Study 2008* (Northbrook, IL: Research International USA, 2007).

5. Check out these Web sites to see if there is a chapter in your teen's local school:

Young Life, www.younglife.org

Fellowship of Christian Athletes, www.fca.org

First Priority, www.firstpriority.org

6. Beth Moore, *Daniel: Lives of Integrity, Words of Prophecy* (Nashville: Lifeway, 2006), 26.

7. There are several quotes in the recounting of the Daniel story. All the quotes are taken from the New Living Translation, Daniel 1–3.

Chapter 13

1. Anne Lamott, *Plan B: Further Thoughts on Faith* (New York: Riverhead, 2005), 198.

About the Author

Brian has spent the past fifteen years serving in a variety of roles from youth pastor to camp director to school administrator. Presently he serves as the executive director of Awake to Life, a nonprofit organization that exists to challenge people to wake up to the life God has in store for them.

Brian and his wife, Mona, live in Memphis, Tennessee, with their two kids, Bailey and Ashlan, and a dog named Max.

If you would like more information on Awake to Life, or to schedule Brian for a student or family camp, parent conference, PTA/PTF workshop, or teachers' training, visit www.awaketolife.org.